GW00357811

Eleanor Hewardine MBE was born in Belfast in the 1930s and was educated at Methodist College Belfast. During her school career she had a particular interest in languages and intended to go to university to study French and German. Before her final exams she learnt that the only career available with these subjects was teaching which she did not wish to do. After research she discovered that speech therapy was a career which offered an interest in language with medical and psychological input. In 1951 she commenced her training at the Edinburgh School of Speech Therapy.

She had an interesting career working in hospital and community both as a clinician and manager. Following early retirement she set up a voluntary organisation dealing with adults with aphasia.

In 1987 she was awarded the Honours of the College of Speech and Language Therapists, in 1992 she was awarded an MBE for her services to Speech Therapy.

She continues to live in Belfast.

Memoirs of a Peash Ferapis

Eleanor Hewardine MBE

Memoirs of a Peash Ferapis

Vanguard Press

VANGUARD PAPERBACK

A CIP catalogue record for this title is
available from the British Library.

ISBNL: 978-1-84386-780-7

The names and circumstances of those mentioned in this book have been
changed to protect their identities and the terminology used throughout the
book was in vogue when the author was a practicing clinician.

Vanguard Press is an imprint of
Pegasus Elliot Mackenzie Publishers Ltd.
www.pegasuspublishers.com

First Published in 2014

Vanguard Press
Sheraton House Castle Park
Cambridge England

Printed & Bound in Great Britain

This book is dedicated to my dear mother
Jane Scott Hutchinson, whose life was an inspiration
to my family and to me.

Acknowledgements

My thanks to all those who helped me with my book, especially my grandson Gareth Chisholm and Frances Thompson who typed while I dictated, to Alison Downie, Pamela Hardy, Valerie Chisholm and Chris Timney who painstakingly proofread it all, a thankless task. Lastly to Ken Best without whose help and support this book would not have been finished.

However the final book is all my responsibility.

Contents

Foreword

It was at this time that I realised that not only could I not talk – I could not read or write either – what a catastrophe! I could not speak, although my tongue worked perfectly well and I knew what I wanted to say. I could not always fully understand what people said to me, although I was not the slightest bit deaf; I could not read, although I could see words quite clearly on the page – they had no meaning; I could not write, although by this time I had learnt to use a pencil with my left hand – I could in fact copy-write beautifully. As with my speech, I knew what I wanted to write but I could not find the words, and even when I could, I could not spell them.

This passage, written by a stroke victim, illustrates the effect of a communication disorder on an adult.

Children and adults with speech and language problems cannot speak up for themselves and express their anger and frustrations about being unable to communicate effectively.

Speech therapy today is very different to what it was when I qualified over fifty years ago. The College of Speech Therapists was only formed in 1945. Graduates were awarded an LCST (Licentiate of the College of Speech Therapists). Today all graduates have a university degree in that subject and they have to be state registered. Even our name has changed, we are now known as Speech and Language Therapists.

The names and circumstances of those mentioned in this book have been changed to protect their identities and the terminology used throughout the book was in vogue when I was a practising clinician.

1

Belfast Here I Come L.C.S.T. 1954

Belfast here I come! – That was the telegram I sent to my mother from the college in Edinburgh on the day I received my exam results. My mother read the LCST as being 'lost' and she rushed to tell my grandmother that I had failed my exams! My grandmother, however, looked at the telegram and said, "I think you've got it wrong dear, I think she's passed!"

So here I was, aged twenty-one, a fully qualified speech therapist, a Licentiate of the College of Speech Therapists, looking forward to my first post. My interview at the Royal Group of Hospitals was just two weeks away.

I was slightly apprehensive as a few months earlier I had had my oral exam in phonetics. There I was, in my new navy and white dress bought especially for the occasion, waiting for my turn to be called. I was the seventh out of the nine students so I had quite a wait. When I was called I got up quickly, heard an ominous sound of something tearing. My dress had caught on a nail on the chair and there was a huge rip down the back of my skirt. What could I do? I had to go on for my oral, and as I walked down towards the examiners at the desk at the bottom of the room, all I was thinking of was how am I going to get out of here with a tear in my dress and my underwear on show.

I don't know what the examiners must have thought about me as I left the room backwards!

A few weeks later I had my interview at the Sick Children's Hospital Belfast. I was delighted to hear that I had been successful.

I started work in September of that year.

2

What's That Dear?

I became a speech therapist almost by accident, a career that I enjoyed both as a clinician and as a manager until I took early retirement from the health service in 1991. Following this I set up a charity dealing with adults suffering from aphasia, a speech and language disorder that can follow a stroke or head injury.

Events in our early childhood often have a great effect on what happens to us in the future. I was an only child. My mother had two babies after me, both were stillborn. A few years later she had another baby boy who lived until he was thirteen months old and died following convulsions. It was only when my mother died aged eighty-seven that we discovered during her last illness that she was Rhesus Negative. It was a condition no one knew about in the 1930s and this was most likely the cause of all the stillbirths.

We lived next door to my grandmother and grandfather. My grandmother had rheumatoid arthritis and was unable to walk. During the blitz it was very difficult to move her. She had a bedroom on the ground floor but she had to be lifted and taken to a place of safety. After the second blitz my grandfather decided that it would be better for us to live somewhere other than the city. He took a little cottage in the country about twelve miles away and so I attended school there for a few months.

I don't remember much about my life in the country except that I loved being there. I loved going to help the farmer to bring the cows in and really enjoyed going to the farmer's wife and helping her when she was making soda bread or potato bread. I do have one other memory – a sad one. I think my father must have been on leave before going overseas but the only thing I remember is sitting on a dry stone wall and my father saying to me, "You will look after your mummy Ellie won't you?" and I said, "Yes I will Daddy."

Memory is very selective and I don't remember very much more about that time. My next memory is probably about six or eight months later – we were back living in Belfast again.

It was, I think, a Saturday evening. My mother was in hospital and my grandmother was getting me ready for bed. There was a knock on the door, my grandfather answered, and came back into the room with a man. He spoke with my grandmother and I was then sent into another room. The following day some relatives came to the house and my grandfather took me on his knee to tell me my father was dead. He had been killed on active service in North Africa.

I don't know if I realised that at the same time my mother was seriously ill in hospital, having just lost another baby. Losing two children and my father in a period of fourteen months had a profound effect on my mother. I think she was determined that I, as an only child, should consequently have the best of everything. I was sent to elocution and music lessons and then I was sent off to a prep school. This is the part where I think my life actually changed, although I did not realise this until many years later.

My best subject in school was mathematics; however, in my new school I was to find another love. I came home from school after my first few days there full of excitement, to tell my mother that we were learning French and asked her if she knew that in France things are either ladies or men (as a child this was my attempt at describing masculine and feminine). A few years later in school I studied Latin and I enjoyed that as well. I had discovered a new interest, languages.

When I was aged thirteen I went into the senior school and a teacher came round to ask, "Eleanor, do you want to do Arts or Sciences?"

I asked what that meant! I was told that if I did Arts I would be able to take up German as an additional subject and if I did sciences I would have to do physics, chemistry and biology. The only thing I knew about sciences was the fact that the laboratories had an awful smell and were mostly very dull, grey and black. In my mind there was absolutely no choice, I opted for Arts.

I continued my school career, and eventually, in my final year I decided that I was going to go to university to study languages. That was as far ahead as I thought at that time. About three months before my final exams a friend in school asked me what I was going to do and I told her I was going to university to study languages.

"I didn't think you wanted to be a teacher?" she said.

"I don't want to be a teacher; I couldn't bear the thought of being a teacher!" I replied.

Her response was, "What else can you do with a language degree?"

I went home and as usual discussed this with my mother. We thought about all the different careers I could do. However,

21

for most of the careers we thought about I would have needed science. Fate took a hand again! A few months previously there had been an invitation on the school notice board saying that if anyone was interested in speech therapy, they could come to see a speech therapist at work. I had put my name down to go, but unfortunately that morning I had a hockey match to attend.

So I came into school and asked if anyone had heard about speech therapy and someone told me, "You wouldn't want to do that, you have to put your fingers in children's mouths."

However, I went home and again asked my mother about it. She phoned her GP and asked him. He replied, as I think most GPs would have then, that he knew nothing about speech therapy but he did know the speech therapist at the hospital.

So the following Saturday morning I went to the hospital and saw a speech therapist at work. That was when I decided what I wanted to do. I came home and told my mother that I wanted to be a speech therapist.

"What's that dear?" was her reply.

3

College Years 1951 – 1954

I went ahead and applied to Edinburgh School of Speech Therapy which was affiliated to Edinburgh University. I travelled over to have my interview and just a few weeks later I was told I'd been accepted and that I would start my course in October that year.

When I started at the college there were only ten students in our year. The first morning was quite exciting. I arrived at a tall and imposing terraced building in a picturesque part of the city. I went down to the basement where the meeting was to be held. At the bottom of the steps there were a number of girls standing around. They were third year students. They all looked beautiful and well-dressed. I think all of the new students were in awe of them.

During our introductory meeting that morning, our Director of Studies told us that for our first day we would only be there for an hour. She gave us a timetable for the rest of the week and told us we would be there at the college only a few hours each week. The rest of the time would be spent at the University. We were also told that each week we would have a nail inspection and we should use deodorant every day because the room was quite small and she didn't want us to smell! It was a very different approach to what happens today.

The subjects we were studying were mainly speech pathology and therapeutics – the different disorders of speech and language and how to treat them. One of our first assignments was to have a weekly visit to a nursery school. This was not only to give us experience of working with young children, but it also allowed us to listen to their speech and language and to observe their motor developments.

On the first day I went down to the nursery with a fellow student, Ann. The head teacher greeted us and said, "I am so glad to see you arriving; we have very many children here this year with speech problems. I will send them in."

Ann and I looked at each other in amazement; we did not know anything about speech and language problems at that point. We decided that the only thing we could do that first morning was to take the names of the children and each week after that attempt to treat them with what we were learning in our lectures. At that time the only thing we were doing was 'articulation exercises', i.e. exercises for the tongue, lips and palate. So over the next number of weeks those poor children came in and had their tongues, lips and palates exercised. We didn't know anything else to do. I would say that within five weeks they had the best articulatory organs in the country.

Another subject I studied at University was psychology, I found this fascinating and I thoroughly enjoyed my lectures. For example, we were told that children who suck their thumbs are deprived of love! During my early years of practice I used to look at these children coming in sucking their thumbs, thinking that I understood why they did so. However when my daughter was born some years later, a much wanted child, she was placed in my arms with her thumb in her mouth, so that was one rapidly disproven theory! Our lecturer was very avant-garde and told us that when her children were born she had put them in the bath to see if they made swimming movements, to test the theory that we were descended from fish, or put a stick in their hands to grasp then lifted them up, to test if we were descended from apes! I didn't try that with my children!

We studied anatomy and physiology which I enjoyed. The first year was all theory. In our second year the new lecturer decided that just learning anatomy and physiology was not enough and he thought we should actually see a body to understand it. So the following week we all went to the dissecting lab. It was absolutely awful! There was a body lying on the table. It had gone completely black. The various internal organs were lying on top of it and the smell in the room was horrific. I realised I could never have been a doctor or a nurse.

That day we had to study the brain and while I felt quite queasy, it was not until later when I arrived home to see that dinner included cauliflower in cheese sauce that I really was sick. I could not look at cauliflower for years afterwards.

One day our anatomy lecturer informed us that over the next few weeks we would be going in pairs to observe cleft-palate and harelip operations. We were told that we were definitely not to wear anything nylon as the operating theatre was very warm and that if we felt faint we were to get out of the room as quickly as possible. On the afternoon I was scheduled to go, I kept saying to myself, "If you feel faint just remember, look at something else, do not watch the operation, do not faint, whatever you do, do not faint."

I arrived at the Sick Children's Hospital, went up to the operating room and put on my gown and went in. I was standing right next to the surgeon on his left-hand side. He then apologised that the patient with cleft-palate was unfortunately sick and he was going to do a skin graft instead. The child was wheeled into theatre and the surgeon took up the scalpel, drew a little line down the girl's arm. Tiny droplets of blood appeared. The next thing I knew I was sitting outside the operating theatre in a corridor! I don't remember how I got there.

While I was sitting there giving off to myself, a cot was wheeled in beside me. In it there lay this baby with the hare lip. You can imagine how much of a shock it was for any mother to see her child like that. When this operation was to take place I went back into the theatre. I suppose because I was so interested in what they were going to do I managed to watch the whole operation without fainting. The transformation in the child was wonderful, just a tiny row of stitches in place of the gaping hole.

We studied neurology for over two years, a most interesting subject. I don't think students do that amount of neurology in the training college these days, in fact in our third year we sat in with the postgraduate medical students every Friday afternoon. One of our clinical medical officers in later years was quite astounded at the amount of neurology I actually knew.

One of the main subjects at that time was normal voice and speech. During every lecture we practised tongue twisters like 'red leather, yellow leather', and 'mixed biscuits in a big mixed biscuit box'. We also learnt a lot of the verses from Gilbert and Sullivan, for example 'what a to-do to die today', or 'I am the very model of a modern Major General'. We had to articulate these very clearly, enunciating each word perfectly.

We did Chinese whispers, talk for a minute, we listened to nonsense words etc. Quite understandable when you think that we were actually in a school of speech and drama! None of this is done in training schools today.

In preparation for our future work with stammerers, we studied relaxation. We used the Jacobsen Method. During this we would all lie on the floor. Our Director of Studies would go through the work starting with our head. This would be, tighten your eyes, relax, tighten your face, relax. She would then work down to our neck, arms, body, legs and right down to our feet. Then, as we all lay there, she would start speaking in a very calm voice and say something like, "It's a warm sunny day; you are lying on the beach. Relax, relax into the sand. Feel the sun on your body. Relax, relax."

We would all lie there enjoying the rest.

One day we were doing this in the hospital, I was beautifully relaxed and I began imagining that I was lying on the beach with the sun shining on me. When somebody opened the door behind me and hit me on the head! It was a shock! It was the last time I ever relaxed near a door!

Another part of this subject was mime and movement. This class was held every Monday afternoon at two o'clock and I dreaded it. I was always very tall; I was by far the tallest in the group of students. I hated being told to be a tree in the wind, having to stand there waving my arms in the air was awful. The worst was the time I was expected to be a dying duck in a snowstorm. How do you, at five foot seven and a half, pretend to be a duck dying in a snowstorm? I cannot tell you how delighted I was when that particular course ended.

Phonetics posed quite a problem. In Northern Ireland we do have a funny system with our vowels. Most Northern Irish students going across to England or Scotland to do speech therapy had great difficulty with phonetics. For example in Northern Ireland 'flower' is pronounced 'flar', 'tower' is pronounced 'tar' and some people even pronounce Northern Ireland as 'Norn Iron'! Train is pronounced 'tree-in', 'plane is pronounced 'plee-in', bag is pronounced 'bye-g', etc.

One of the exercises we did was to have our voices taped. Having done elocution for nearly ten years, I did not think that I had an accent. However, when the tapes were played back and I heard the Irish voice, I said, "Who's that?" and of course everyone laughed and said, "That's you!" I couldn't believe I did sound so Irish! When we eventually left Edinburgh we all spoke what is known as 'received pronunciation' i.e. BBC English, not one of us had an accent.

About six months after I returned home. I went back to visit friends and took my Director of Studies out for lunch. Her comment to me:

"Eleanor, I don't know why we bothered, you're as Irish as ever!"

4

My First Post 1954

When I first qualified aged twenty-one and returned to Belfast to work I was very fortunate that I managed to secure a post working in a hospital. The majority of therapists who qualified at that time went to work in the community. Working in the hospital meant that I had a senior therapist who was there to provide help and support. This was something that those who went into the community did not have.

At that time we all worked a thirty-three hour week. It was a very strange arrangement because I worked from half past nine to half past twelve, had an hour and a half for lunch, and started again from two o'clock until five. I also worked on Saturday mornings. My week was made up of eight sessions with children, two sessions of working in the nearby hospital outpatient department and in the wards with inpatients and one session in the evening working in a hospital for people with neurological problems.

I really loved the work. The only thing I was not very happy about was the work with inpatients and outpatients with aphasia, a speech and language disorder as a result of stroke or head injury. I think the reason that I did not like this work was the fact that at the time we had no test materials, we had to make up our own. I feel at that time I was not particularly confident about what I was doing. It is ironic that in later years I actually set up a charity dealing with patients with aphasia.

One of the first patients I treated when I started working in the hospital was a child aged five named Jane Ross. Jane had a severe speech and language disorder. One of the first lessons that we as speech therapists were taught to do was to get to know the family of the patient very well, and so I learned all about Jane and her early history.

Mrs Ross had been married and discovered that she was pregnant shortly after her husband joined the army at the start of the war. She decided that rather than setting up home and waiting for her husband to return, she and the baby would stay at home with her parents, brothers and sisters. This she did until the war was over and her husband eventually returned home. A year later her second child, a daughter, Jane, was born. By which time they had bought their own house and for the first time in her life Mrs Ross was responsible for running a home.

Mrs Ross was a delightful lady. Unfortunately she had a very big problem; she could never say no to anyone. For example, the woman next door would say, "Are you going to do your shopping? Can you bring me back some meat and I'll pay you when you come back?" Mrs Ross would do it and of course her neighbour never did pay. Mrs Ross' brother ran a little scout troop every Saturday and after playing football they would all come back with dirty uniforms. He would come to his sister and ask her to wash these for him as his wife wouldn't. Needless to say, she complied.

So each week when Mrs Ross came, she would tell me what had been happening to her during the week. One day I discovered that because of all these difficulties she had spoken to a doctor who had referred her for counselling. Every week we chatted a little more about her problems and in the course of one of our conversations I discovered that a few years previously she had had a quarrel with her husband following which she had taken her clothes and moved into the spare room. She never returned to share the room with Mr Ross. I asked her if she had told the counsellor this and she said, "Oh no, I couldn't tell him that."

In my naivety I thought this was terrible. I said to Mrs Ross that this was an awful thing to do and that she must go home right away and move back in with her husband. I finished my work for the day, went home and didn't spare another thought about what I'd said.

The following afternoon I was sitting at my desk when there was a loud knock on the door. I called "Come in," and a tall gentleman entered. He walked over to my desk.

"Miss Hutchinson?" he asked.

"Yes," I replied.

"My name is Ross." I looked up at him. I thought, *Oh my goodness, what have I done!*

I could feel my heart thumping, I was terrified, I thought he was going to make a complaint. I had visions of losing my job and I had only just started! However, he leaned over my desk, shook my hand, and said, "Miss Hutchinson, you're a very sensible young woman."

I became very friendly with the family and continued to see them over the next number of years.

This aspect of the work, i.e. the counselling, led to a very interesting career. During my time at the hospital I changed some of my treatment methods and even introduced some of my own ideas.

During my training in Edinburgh the Director of Studies did not like us to have parents coming in and sitting there while we were treating their child. I can remember during the oral part of my final exams, when I was treating a patient, the examiner asked me why I did not have the parent in the room. Of course I quoted all we had been taught: e.g. how the parents were inclined to interfere and children co-operated better without the parent there.

So, abiding by my training, I began work and didn't allow parents to sit in with me during the treatment of the child. However, I learnt an invaluable lesson while treating one of my first patients, a little boy named Tommy who had a cleft palate. Today we very seldom hear of children or adults with a cleft palate, the operative techniques have improved so much. When I started work it was quite common to hear people with cleft palate speech. They would speak 'through the nose', i.e. have very nasal speech, but Tommy did not. His main problem was that he just could not make any consonants, in place of them he would make an 'ugh' sound, so when he would say 'apple tart', it would come out as 'ah-ugh-ah'.

I began Tommy's treatment, with one of the earliest sounds to develop being the 'p'. I spent a lesson showing him how to do this and then to join the sound with a vowel. I put a piece of paper on the back of my hand, so that when he would say 'p' the paper would blow away. Then he would have to say 'p-ha', 'p-hee', and so on, so that eventually he could join the consonant and vowel to say 'pa' and 'pee' etc.

After the lesson I went outside to speak to his mother to tell her how to do it and off they went. The following week she returned with Tommy. I brought him into the room and he could not do it. I went over the lesson again and afterwards I spoke to his mother again. "You know, you really do need to practise with Tommy every day, just five minutes at a time is all you need," I told her. She assured me that she had indeed practised every day.

I was dubious about this, so I reiterated what she had to do. The following week Tommy returned, but still couldn't say 'pa', 'pee' etc. So Miss Know-It-All brought his mother into the room and asked her to show me how she did it.

She said, "Tommy say 'pee-ah'," which of course he couldn't do, as he was still learning to join the consonant to the vowel. She was not meant to say 'pee', just to make the sound of the letter 'p', followed by an 'ee'. I suddenly realised that I had spent three years learning how to do this and had expected her to learn it in five minutes at the end of a lesson. So she sat in with us, I showed her what to do and the following week Tommy returned and was 'pa' 'pee' perfect. I have to report that once Tommy learned to use the 'p' he did wonderfully well and was able to be discharged in a very short time.

From then on I always had the parent in with me while treating their child. The one exception being a boy named Austin. Every Tuesday morning I would get a bad feeling when preparing for work. Austin was the problem! I love children, I never lose patience with them, but Austin defeated me. I would never allow his mother into the room during our session, as she would continuously interrupt, demanding, "Austin, say that again," or interjecting, "Don't do that Austin." Understandably, I had to keep her outside.

Austin would come in and I would try chatting to him, but instead of responding he would simply glare at me. I tried everything I could think of to engage with him, but nothing worked. Eventually I would say, "Can you get your book out now?" at which point he would open his school bag to bring out his speech book, slam it down on the table and say, "Oh God!"

I was glad when I eventually discharged him with normal speech, my Tuesday mornings improved!

The following case taught me a treatment regime which I was to carry out with great success in later years. A ten-year-old girl from the North Coast was referred to the hospital for treatment. She had quite a severe speech defect. Her mother had to get a lift to take her six miles to the nearest train station to begin her journey to Belfast. She then had a further bus journey to where she would get another bus to bring her to the hospital. All in all she would have to spend around four hours travelling each way to get therapy. What could I do to improve this arrangement? The child needed treatment but obviously the mother could not spend eight hours travelling each week to receive it. It's hard to believe now but when I qualified as a speech therapist there were only five of us in the whole of Ireland.

I asked the mother if she had any relatives or friends who lived in Belfast. She told me that her sister lived nearby. So I sent her off to ask her sister if she would be prepared to look after the child for one or two weeks and I would provide treatment every day for that period. The mother returned shortly afterwards to say that her sister was delighted to help. So the mother went home that day without her daughter and I arranged for her to come in every day for treatment. Her aunt worked well with her and at the end of two weeks the child's speech was almost normal. I suddenly realised the value of intensive therapy.

The following case which deals with an adult reinforced my belief in this type of treatment. This concerned a lady in her early thirties who had had a massive stroke about eight years previously. When I met her the only things she could say were 'aye, aye, aye', and 'no, no, no'. Her husband very often came with her. They had to come by ambulance because she lived about twelve miles away.

During one of our treatment sessions she pointed to my name badge and said, "Aye, aye, aye." Her husband then said, "She wants to know what the 'E' stands for?"

In those days a patient would never have thought of calling a therapist by her first name and I would never have thought of calling her by her first name either. How times have changed!

When I told her it stood for Eleanor, she said, "Aye, aye, aye," and her husband explained to me that it was her name too. When she was a child her younger brother was unable to say it. He always called her 'Nora', at which point her husband went on to say that in fact her younger brother was the only other one in the family who was left-handed as she was. Mrs Boyd had right-sided hemiplegia and in those days we assumed that the language centre was situated in the dominant side of the brain. She was left-handed; therefore we would assume that her language centre would be situated in the right-hand side of the brain.

I couldn't understand this because if she had a right hemiplegic, the left-hand side of her brain was damaged and I thought how could she possibly be aphasic? So I decided that could not be the problem.

The following day I went to speak to her consultant, Dr Calvert, and I said that I didn't believe that Mrs Boyd was actually aphasic. I asked him if he would allow me to bring her into the hospital for two weeks of intensive therapy. He agreed and both she and her husband were delighted at the thought that something might be done.

The following week she came into hospital and every morning I went to see her. I would be there at nine o'clock for her treatment, come back to treat my other patients, go over again at lunchtime and if someone missed their appointment for the afternoon session I'd go back over to her again. I enlisted the help of any patient in the ward who was able to speak and I depended on the nurses too. I'm pleased to say that when Mrs Boyd left the hospital she was beginning to say quite a few words.

The day she left, I received a phone call from her husband. During the time she had been in hospital I had been reporting to him on her good progress, but obviously when he arrived she was too excited to demonstrate this and didn't say anything. He was crying over the phone. He said, "Miss Hutchinson, I never thought I would hear Nora talking again, but when we got home she said, 'Put kettle on, starving!'"

I treated Mrs Boyd until I left the hospital and I heard that she continued to improve.

When I started my charity in 1991 I organised intensive courses for patients with aphasia. It was wonderful.

5

Community Work 1957 – 1974.
A Time of Change

I worked at the hospital for the next eighteen months and then I got married. As I suppose was usual in those days, my husband expected me to be at home so I handed in my resignation. However, to my surprise, my senior therapist asked me if I would consider staying on for at least two sessions a week to finish working with my current patients. I agreed and I ended up staying on for a further eight months then resigned to be a full time housewife and eventually a mother when my son was born.

Less than a year later when my son was four months old I was contacted by the Senior Medical Officer for Belfast School Health Services. He asked me if I would do some sessions at a local clinic. The community clinic he was suggesting was only a mile away from my home, so it would be very handy if I decided to accept his offer.

I said, "No, I couldn't possibly consider work while I have a young baby." However, a few days later as I was washing nappies (no Pampers in those days) it occurred to me that it might make a welcome change! I asked my mother if she would be prepared to mind David (my son) for two afternoons a week. She agreed and I began work at the community clinic. I said that I would do it for three months initially. I actually stayed for the next thirty-four years!

My first day in my position was very unusual for me, as I had never worked in a community clinic before. I was introduced to the staff. I met the clinical medical officers, the health visitors and clerical staff. The health visitors were wonderful people. They knew the schools very well and I could always find out from them about problem families. The system they operated on at that time assigned every child a folder. In it were coloured cards relating to different problems e.g. a beige coloured card related to hearing defects, a green card for a visual defect and a yellow card for a speech problem. On my first day I was handed a pile of them, around twenty-five or thirty. I was told they represented the children currently waiting for treatment. I didn't think that was very many so I made appointments to interview them.

Some of these children had been referred as far back as ten years previously but had never been seen by a therapist and naturally some of them did not turn up. The children who did turn up were seen, assessed and advised, or taken on for treatment. I felt very satisfied. I thought I had dealt with all of the referrals. A few weeks later I was astounded to be handed a further pile of yellow cards, one hundred and thirty-eight in number! The staff at the clinic had sent all the yellow cards to the hospital to see if any of the children were currently on the waiting list there. Unfortunately, none of them were and the cards had been returned.

I'm sure you can imagine how hard it was to cope with this sheer number of referrals as I had already taken patients on for treatment for my two afternoons.

This continued for two years, until I was pregnant again. I remember one afternoon one of the Clinical Medical Officers asked me when the baby was due.

"Four weeks," I replied.

"Well, I just want you to know," she said, "it's been a long time since Dr Campbell or I did any maternity work."

I took the hint and stopped working the following week, although I did manage to get back just a month after the birth.

I continued my work at the clinic on two afternoons a week for the next four years until both my son and daughter were at school. I decided it would be better if I took them to school in the morning, went to the clinic straight from there and was home for lunchtime.

I didn't work school holidays at all in those days, but I was under constant pressure to do extra sessions. Gradually I took on one more, then another and another and so on until by 1970 I was working twenty-one hours a week, in the mornings and finishing at lunchtime except for Mondays when I left at 3.00 p.m.

Sometime after I had increased my sessions I was asked to see the senior clinical medical officer. He wanted to tell me that he had just been informed that a full time speech therapist had been appointed to Belfast School Health Service and she would be coming to do two sessions each week at our clinic. I was delighted. Additional help at last!

For sometime Dr Campbell had been trying to persuade me to do a session or two each week at a school for children who were 'slow learners' (in old terminology an ESN school). This type of school would now be deemed a Resource Centre.

I was always reluctant to take on an extra commitment when I felt I was already over-stretched with the caseload I had.

However, now I had been told additional assistance was available I agreed.

A few weeks later I started doing one session a week in the school. There were a large number of children needing therapy. Initially I assessed all those who were referred, prioritised them and then started treatment.

The school staff were all very friendly and I enjoyed my time there.

The room which I used was enormous. It had been one of the attics in the house and a teacher actually used the adjoining room as a classroom. There was only a small gas fire at one end and one small window. When it rained the water often came in through the cracks and would lie on the floor. However, this did not bother me as speech therapists were used to working in such unsuitable places.

In order to save myself running up and down three flights of stairs each time I wanted to see a child I would bring up two or three at a time. One morning I was treating a child when suddenly a girl ran up and said, "Hey Miss, Sadie Brown is chewing gum."

Before I could say anything Sadie came up and said, "No, I was not – you're telling lies."

Now, she was so close to me I could smell the mint. So I said, "Sadie I can smell the chewing gum and I don't mind you chewing it but I don't want you telling me lies."

Up went her arm in the air. "Declare to God Miss, I was not chewing gum. I was chewing gum last night and I have a hole in my tooth – some of it must have got stuck there and that is what you smell." How was that for an impromptu excuse from a 'slow learner'?

A sad boy I met there was called Richard. He was a tall good looking boy who never seemed to laugh, he just looked so sad all the time. He always came over to see me when I came in. His mother came for an interview. She was so pleased to be seeing a therapist as she had wanted him to have treatment for a long time.

The story was as follows. Richard's early development was excellent. He walked and talked very early. He was able to read a little by the time he was three years of age. Then his mother noticed that he seemed to quieten down and she felt that he was not progressing as he had done. He was seen by a doctor and then by a psychologist. Richard was assessed and his mother was told that he had an IQ of 100 – much lower that anyone would have expected. He was reviewed again a year later and the IQ given at that time was 80. Obviously something had happened. The family were living abroad at that time but shortly after returned to Northern Ireland. I cannot remember now if Richard was seen by any other doctor when they came home.

After Richard's mother had given me the case history I contacted a neurologist, who I knew was particularly interested in children with speech and language problems. He made an appointment to see Richard. I heard from Mrs Martin later that they had a very long interview and a full assessment, by the end of which the doctor had discovered that at about three years Richard had not been well. He had a raised temperature for a time, nothing his mother felt was serious and she had not been worried about it. The doctor felt that Richard probably had encephalitis at that time which had caused brain damage and that was why he had made no further development.

They were a lovely family and I was sad that I could not have done more to help them. I saw Richard some years later. He was then in a centre for adults with special needs and as before he came over to give me a big hug. He was a lovely boy.

One morning I came into the school to find the secretary Miss Beggs (Bertha) in a great state! Now, I have to explain about Bertha. She was a most efficient secretary and a very friendly person but she did become very excited if things were not going well. In stature she was small and thin but she had a well developed chest which went up and down at an alarming rate when she got excited. That day it was jumping! The reason for the excitement was that the previous day one of the senior pupils, a boy of about fifteen had been tragically killed in an accident. The family had contacted the school asking if six of the boys could be pall bearers.

When I arrived Bertha was saying over and over again, "They'll drop him – I know they will – it will be awful – they'll drop him – I know they will." She then pointed out of the window. There was one of the teachers instructing six pupils by making them carry boxes on their shoulders on how they would carry a coffin. They were walking around the school while the teacher called out, "Slowly 123."

There was Bertha, chest jumping up and down, and shouting, "They'll drop him," while these six boys and their teacher were walking round and round the school with boxes on their shoulders. I didn't know how to react.

The funeral went over without any problems. They didn't drop him.

About this time a teenage girl was referred to me. She had a stammer which was quite severe. During the interview it appeared that the problem was that her parents had recently

42

bought a shop and they were expecting her to use the till. Deidre was very good at reading and spelling but she simply could not cope with numbers, so having to use the till was almost impossible for her. In her school she was in the lowest class.

I spoke to one of the educational psychologists who agreed to give Deidre some individual tuition in maths.

I continued to treat Deidre at the clinic. After some time the psychologist asked to see me. She felt that Deidre was not making any progress with numbers and queried what we should do. She suggested that we speak to the parents to see if they would give permission for Deidre to transfer to an ESN school. This was a problem on two counts. One being a transfer from a secondary school to an ESN school would be one which many parents would automatically reject. Secondly the pupils in the ESN School were mainly of a different religion. This can be a problem in Northern Ireland.

The psychologist and I arranged to see the parents and explain the problem. To our surprise the parents agreed right away.

The change in Deidre was wonderful. Firstly, as an excellent reader she was the best in the school and not the worst. She was given duties to do which she enjoyed. Secondly, the fact that her maths was poor did not pose the same problem and as her confidence grew her stammer lessened. She was able to be discharged a short time after that.

Nineteen seventy was a very special year for me, and a number of events happened at that time. First of all, during the previous year a colleague and I had decided it would be a good idea to contact the other speech therapists in Northern Ireland. We didn't know many of them personally, so we contacted those we did and asked them if they knew any others and eventually nineteen therapists from across Northern Ireland arrived at a meeting we'd organised in Belfast.

The therapists came to the decision to meet once every three months, to exchange ideas and provide help and support for each other. We set up a committee. I was asked to be chairman. I declined on the grounds that I knew very little about running a committee and wasn't sure I could do it. Instead I volunteered to be secretary, which I think shows just how little I knew about committees at the time, having volunteered for the post that requires the most work! I did enjoy it however. So in 1970 we had the first meeting of the Irish District of the Scottish area of the College of Speech Therapists, which included therapists from the South of Ireland.

Another exciting event for me that year was when one morning, while sitting in the clinic, I received a call from the Senior Clinical Medical Officer for Belfast School Health Services. He called to tell me that, at a meeting the Health Committee the previous evening, a motion had been proposed and passed that I would become the Senior Speech Therapist for Belfast. He told me I would be the first part-time officer to be offered a senior post. I was quite thrilled! At that time my staff consisted of one full-time and two other part-time staff in addition to myself.

In 1970 physiotherapists and occupational therapists at a local hospital decided that they no longer wanted to be included in the Whitley Council, which granted payments of salaries and conditions of service for professions supplementary to medicine and speech therapists. They wanted to withdraw from that so they set up meetings to discuss the issues. The senior speech therapist at the hospital was asked if she would attend and she did, for one meeting only. At that first meeting she decided that she could not go back again, as speech therapy was not deemed to be a profession supplementary to medicine, she felt that she shouldn't be present.

Soon afterwards, at a meeting of speech therapists in Dungannon, I was asked if I would go in her place. The reason there was doubt over our profession attending was that in 1959 the College of Speech Therapists had succeeded in having our profession removed from the Professions Supplementary to Medicine, arguing correctly that we form our own diagnoses. The Whitley Council Agreement in which we were included read 'Professions Supplementary to Medicine and Speech Therapy'.

The college of Speech Therapists agreed I could attend as an observer, only I was not supposed to participate. This group became the Paramedical Advisory Committee and I soon realised that very interesting things were happening. I contacted the College of Speech Therapists to let them know I would be attending and that I'd keep them informed of any decisions made but I would not merely observe. I would actively participate in all the discussions.

The most exciting change that was happening as a result of this committee was the proposed establishment of the new physiotherapy and occupational therapy training courses at Jordanstown Polytechnic. I felt that we also needed a speech therapy training school and due to my involvement with the Paramedical Liaison Committee, this was set up and in 1975 the first students were accepted, ten in number, five of whom were on bursaries from Eastern Board.

6

Senior Speech Therapist

When I became the senior speech therapist for Belfast in 1970 I had three therapists working in Belfast as well as myself, only one of these was full-time. When I first started work in the community clinic in East Belfast in 1957, one of my main aims was to train health visitors in what to look for when they were assessing a child with a speech and language problem or a stammer. One of my first aims when I took the senior post was to continue this programme across the other clinical areas of Belfast. The second arrangement I made was for the four of us to meet every few months for a staff meeting. This was very important at that time when therapists were working in isolation as these meetings provided help and support.

There were no published test materials at that time, so when a child came in for assessment we listened to what they were saying and then wrote it down phonetically. With regard to a language assessment the same thing applied, we wrote down what the child was saying and devised a programme from that. It certainly wasn't scientific but it was all we had.

In 1972 I heard that there had been a test published called the Reynell Test, so I decided that I would try and organise a demonstration of this for my staff and others in Northern

Ireland. I contacted the therapist and the psychologist in England who demonstrated the test and they agreed to come over to Belfast.

On the morning in question, a colleague and I went to the train station to meet the lecturers. They had been demonstrating the test in Dublin the previous day. We went straight up to the clinic where the other therapists were waiting. Unfortunately the lecturers discovered that the video which they had brought to demonstrate the test was no longer working. I was asked if there would be a child of between four to six years of age in the clinic who would be willing to participate. I went to investigate, however, that morning there were no children in the clinic at all. I went and spoke to the health visitors, one of whom suggested we try a local school, so off we went. Unfortunately there were no parents with children around that morning and naturally the school would not allow us to take one of the children from the classroom without their parent's consent. So what were we to do? The health visitor and I got into the car and headed back into the clinic. As we drove along we suddenly saw a mother standing at her door, arms akimbo, watching two young girls playing on the pavement. So I stopped the car and the health visitor and I looked at each other.

"What age do you think those children are?" I asked.

She replied, "Hmm, about three or four? That sort of age maybe."

"What do you think then?" I asked.

"It's worth a try," she replied.

So, we got out of the car, went across the road, explained to the mother what had happened and asked if we could 'borrow' the older child to demonstrate the test. Her reply was, "Of course dear, would you like to take the other one as well?"

Could you imagine such a thing today? However, in Northern Ireland in those days, apart from 'The Troubles', it was a very safe place for children. I don't remember hearing of anything such as child abduction. I told the mother that the health visitor would bring the children back at about 12.30 p.m., and she waved us off quite happily. I think maybe she was glad of a free morning! I organised for the health visitor to collect the children and asked her to get some sweets for them and a box of chocolates for the mother. This she agreed to do. Both children co-operated very well for the test, and at 12.30 p.m. we broke up for lunch.

What happened later was quite a shock for our lecturers. As we came down to the main road, there in front of us, was a bus that had been hijacked and set on fire. It was blazing merrily, the police, fire brigade, etc were all there, plus the usual crowd of bystanders. That evening worse was to come! We had arranged for a dinner to be held at a nearby hotel that night and we all congregated there at seven o'clock.

As the meal progressed we could hear shooting and the occasional bomb and at nine o'clock the manager came and spoke to me and said, "If there is anyone needing to travel across town they would need to leave now, things is very bad tonight."

I heard later, through the grapevine, that the two lecturers said they were terrified and on no account would they ever come back to Belfast. What they didn't know, or at least I don't think they did, was that the following week the hotel was actually blown up!

The second very interesting thing which happened between 1970 and 1971 was that a speech therapy training course had started in Dublin. I received a letter from the College of Speech Therapists asking if I would be willing to serve as an examiner for the College in Dublin. I was very surprised at this but agreed. My colleague from County Fermanagh was also asked to be an examiner. I must say I thoroughly enjoyed my trips down to Dublin which I did for the next few years until the speech therapy course was set up in Northern Ireland and I began examining the students there.

Over the next two years I acquired another two full-time members of staff, which led to a tremendous improvement in the services we were able to offer. I also organised for one of the existing full-time members of staff to be upgraded to take responsibility for the ESN Schools in Belfast.

'The Troubles'

It is hard to know what to say about 'The Troubles' in Northern Ireland over the past number of years as I think enough has been written about this. During the worst time which started about 1968, it was very difficult at times for therapists to get to work and for patients to get to the clinics. During this time there were many casualties who had severe speech and language problems which therapists had to treat. So instead of elaborating these points I will go on to tell you of two amusing incidents which occurred.

One morning there were road blocks everywhere. I started to go to the clinic but my usual route was barred. I tried another way and still could not get through. I then tried to return to my original route but it was impossible. I ended up doing a detour around Belfast of about twelve miles. As I was coming back by a completely different route I thought I would manage to get home without any more trouble. Unfortunately about a mile from my home I ran into another road block. As I approached it I suddenly realised that I had changed my handbag that morning and I had no pass with me. When I arrived at the barrier I was asked for identification. I pulled out my purse wondering if I had anything to show who I was. What came out as I rummaged around was my husband's library card which said 'Dr Shaw'.

"Oh, you're a doctor," the man said, as he peered over my shoulder.

"Open up and let the doctor through."

As it opened up I said a silent prayer, "Please don't let someone have a heart attack, or someone go into labour until I get away."

My prayer was answered.

The second incident involved our car. One morning my husband went off to do his house calls as usual – I tided up the breakfast dishes and left to go to the clinic. When I came out there was no car outside. My husband (a lovely, absent minded professor type) had taken my car and had not noticed that his car was not there. He found my car, a mini, much easier to drive round the streets and was inclined to take it. I stood outside in the driveway pondering, "Where was the car? What had I done with it? Where had I left it the day before?"

It took me a long time to realise that the car had probably been stolen. I came into the house, gave details to the police, phoned Rupert to tell him what had happened and took a taxi down to the clinic.

Anyone reading this who is a golf addict, or who is married to one, will realise the disaster of Rupert's car having being stolen. His golf clubs were in the boot! A calamity!

That evening we were watching the news on television when it was reported that a blue Ford Consul was parked in town and police and army were there as they suspected there was a bomb in it. Rupert immediately thought it was his car and got me to phone and check the registration number. As I did so I had visions of me going to the police and asking if I could get the golf clubs out of the car before they blew it up. Thank goodness it wasn't our car.

7

Personal Note

On a personal note, I continued to play golf two afternoons a week. I was delighted that by the end of 1973 my handicap had come down to twelve and I was very hopeful of getting down to single figures the following year. I was very much a fair-weather golfer and usually stopped playing at the end of September and started again the following April. During the summer months my husband and I would play every other Saturday evening, weather permitting. Thirty-five years ago doctors were still on call at nights and at weekends. They also did maternity cases. When it was Rupert's weekend on, we could not stray far from home.

The other hobby that I really enjoyed was rubber bridge which I played one evening a week. My husband and I were both 'home birds' and did not usually go out very much.

There was a major reorganisation of the Health Service in 1973. In Northern Ireland it was decided that social services were to be included, this was not the case in other parts of the UK. It was to be the Health and Personal Social Services. Northern Ireland was being divided into four Area Boards; each Board would then be divided into a number of Districts. Eastern Board contained 45% of the population of Northern

Ireland. It was the second largest Board in the British Isles, only Glasgow being larger. In January of 1974 the senior personnel officer came to the clinic to inform the staff what these changes were going to mean for our service. He explained that there would be an Area Speech Therapist appointed who would be responsible for all services in Eastern Board. Following the meeting my staff were asking if I was going to apply for the post and I said, "No way!" My post at that time meant I worked mornings only and was finished by one o'clock most days. I didn't work school holidays. (How that came about is another story which I will not go into now.) My husband was a GP and therefore was out each evening at surgery. I felt that if I had a full-time post I would never see him.

However, fate does take a hand in our lives. Four weeks following that meeting, on the 26th January, I was called home from the clinic as my husband had taken ill. I came home to find that he had taken a very severe stroke with a left-sided hemiplegia. He did not want to go into hospital so he had to be nursed at home. It soon became obvious that there was no spontaneous improvement. I was not sure that he would ever get back to work again. I had two teenage children, my salary as the senior speech therapist for Belfast was £20 a week, so I thought that probably wouldn't keep us. I decided I should at least put in an application for the area post.

I was interviewed for this post three months later and was lucky to be successful. Eight months later, in September 1974, I became the Area Speech Therapist for the Eastern Health and Social Services Board (EH and SSB).

My life changed considerably as you can imagine in 1974. My husband did not go into hospital following his stroke but was nursed at home. At that time I was still on my senior speech therapy contract. I worked twenty-one hours per week – all day Monday and mornings only for Tuesday to Friday. I had the school holidays off.

I had an early start every morning – 6.30 a.m. I was up, showered, changed, had my husband dressed, made breakfast for us and my mother and off to work for eight o'clock, then home at lunchtime. I was very fortunate that my mother was able to be there every morning when the physiotherapist came to treat Rupert.

In the afternoon I would spend time going over the physiotherapy exercises and doing all the other duties that were required in a household. Rupert was unable to come downstairs until about three months following his stroke. Until that time we had a private physiotherapist coming in each day. After that he attended the local hospital two hours a week. I no longer played golf.

When, that year, I eventually took up my full-time post things changed again. Obviously I was unable to be there in the afternoon. However, a number of friends would call and take Rupert out for a drive or just call in simply to visit. My mother and the children were there. And so life continued. Rupert eventually was able to walk but had no power in his arm. He eventually got back to work on a part-time basis only – a few hours each week.

Rupert was the youngest of a large family, ten in number. His eldest brother had gone to live in America when Rupert was a child, Harold being nineteen years older than he was. Rupert had only seen him and his wife once in the intervening years. At the end of 1975 he thought he would like to go to Florida to visit Harold and his family. So we started making plans for a two-week holiday in Miami. We were to leave

Belfast on the 12th April 1976. At that time we were still doing the physiotherapy exercises every day. Our evening meal was put back to around six o'clock. Afterwards I tidied up. Then we usually did about two hours of exercises, had some supper and then went to bed. On the fourteenth of March, a Sunday, we were out having a walk; Rupert was in very good form. He still had no power in his left arm but his walking had improved and he was feeling quite optimistic about the future. The following day I was due to have a full staff meeting at the local hospital so wasn't leaving the house just as early as I usually did. I took breakfast up to my mother and to Rupert and came down to have my own breakfast. I went up after that to get dressed and found that Rupert had died. It was a terrible shock.

8

Area Speech Therapist

The reorganisation of the Health and Personal Social Services in Northern Ireland brought great changes. All services became integrated; there were no longer School Health Services, Hospital Services or services for those with Special Needs. Northern Ireland had four Area Boards, the largest of which was the Eastern Board which contained 45% of the population.

It was divided into six Districts: North and West Belfast, South Belfast, East Belfast and Castlereagh, North Down & Ards, Down and Lisburn. When I became Area Speech Therapist in 1974 I had a total of nine staff, 7.5 whole time equivalent (W.T.E) to provide services for over 650,000 of a population.

Eastern Board contained 14 hospitals. The Royal Group had one full-time therapist and there was no service at all in the following hospitals: Belfast City, Ulster, Mater, Musgrave Park, Belvoir Park, Foster Green, Purdysburn, Downe and Downshire, Lagan Valley, Newtownards, Bangor and Muckamore Abbey – a 900 bed facility for people with special needs. For all the special schools and training centres in the Board, the provision at that time was one session per week. So that left the equivalent of just over six speech therapists to cover all the school health services, an impossible task!

Speech therapy (now Speech and Language Therapy) at that time was not highly regarded or even well known. Most people, if you said you were a speech therapist, would say in a very pseudo-posh voice:

"Oh, I will have to speak properly now," or "I will have to speak correctly now."

They obviously thought speech therapy was the same as elocution. This type of comment was infuriating.

The other big problem that I had when I was able to provide a service in clinics was there was no equipment, no test materials, no books, no games, nothing! Speech therapy was not considered a priority. I remember about one year after I became the Area Therapist, being asked to see a teenager who was refusing to go to school. I phoned his nearest clinic and said that I would come and see this boy. I asked if there were any other children they would like me to assess and I would see them when I was there. I enquired if there was a waiting list and was told:

"Yes, the waiting list was closed in 1970 when it reached 400 names."

I went down as arranged to the clinic. To say I was shocked at the problems I discovered there would put it mildly. Of the six or seven children I saw that morning there was one undiagnosed cleft palate, a ten-year-old child with totally unintelligible speech, two five-year-olds who were not talking at all, plus the boy that I had originally gone to see. The education psychologist felt that this boy (Dominic) was refusing to go to school because of his stammer. However, his main problem was that he had quite a severe speech and language disorder, which made his speech almost unintelligible and he was being teased about that.

In light of the number of problems I had seen, I said I would go down once a week to the clinic and start taking some of these children for treatment. I only meant to go there for a short time, but I ended up there for the next six years. So every Wednesday morning I left my house at 7.30 a.m. and headed for the country.

The next big problem I discovered when I went to the clinic was that there were no test materials, no games, or toys, or books, nothing – just a filing cabinet labelled 'speech therapy'. So I made a requisition list and sent it off to the District. I got no reply and assumed that everything had been ordered. A few weeks passed, during which time I had to bring anything I needed from Belfast. I phoned to enquire what had happened to my requisition. Nothing had been ordered! The stock reply was 'there is no money'. So I sent another letter stressing the need for these materials. Again, no reply! At this point I became annoyed; I asked my secretary if she could type a letter with 'HELP, HELP, HELP' written across it in red instead of black and she said she could do this. So a letter something like this was sent:

Dear ....,
HELP, HELP, HELP!
There are currently over 400 children in this District waiting for speech therapy. I have started treating some of them; however, I do not have any test materials, books or equipment. You would not send a doctor to examine a patient without at least a stethoscope, yet you expect me to assess and treat patients without any equipment at all. If I do not receive the

materials I ordered I am afraid I shall have to terminate my visits to this clinic in the near future.

I got my requisition.

One other success story regarding equipment related to the clinic where I had been working since I came to Belfast School Health Services. It was a very old clinic, badly in need of redecoration and with very old desks, chairs, etc. However, at that time that was not my concern. What I really needed when I became the Area Therapist was a filing cabinet. That was all!

I should maybe point out here, how difficult it was when I took up my new post to find out who was responsible for anything. As senior speech therapist for Belfast School Health Services I simply had to liaise with staff at Head Quarters in College Street. As Area Therapist I had to liaise with staff in Area Board which included Area Medical Officers, administration, personnel, supplies, nursing etc. This was then replicated at District level with District Medical Officers etc. So I had to find out whom I needed to talk to in each one of these departments.

For my clinic I eventually found where to go if I wanted a new filing cabinet. As usual the reply was:

"Sorry, there is no money."

However, I talked to the District Supplies Officer and asked him if he had ever been to the clinic. He said, "No," so I invited him over for coffee. He came and I showed him round the clinic. To say he was shocked would maybe be too strong a word, but very shortly after his visit every member of staff got a new desk, a new swivel chair, many of the rooms received new carpets or lino and plans were made to redecorate the clinic in the future.

I got my filing cabinet.

Like everyone else in the clinic I got a new swivel chair to replace my old green iron framed one. I sat on it for a morning then I went out to the back of the clinic and retrieved my old chair. It was much more comfortable.

A number of years later a new health centre was being built and staff from my clinic were being transferred there. When the health visitors and doctors vacated the premises, all the desks and chairs were left behind, too many for my requirements at that time. So, over the next few years when I needed something I operated a barter system.

"I need a filing cabinet, I'll give you a desk," was generally how I went about this. However, this meant the number of desks and chairs were being depleted. One day I went in to one of the clinical rooms and saw a note stuck on top of the desk which said:

"Eleanor, this is my desk. I DO need it, it is not for barter!"

In community clinics throughout the Board there was occasionally accommodation for a speech therapist. Apart from the Royal Victoria Hospital, no provision had ever been made in any other hospital.

Shortly after I took up my post in 1974 I was contacted by a community therapist who told me that her main interest was with adult patients. She was wondering if there was any possibility of providing such a post for her. The next largest hospital to need a therapist was Belfast City, so I went over to see if it would be possible to start a service there. The head of personnel said that there had never been a therapist in the hospital and he queried the need for one! I pointed out that there would definitely be patients with strokes, voice problems, head injuries etc. There was also a children's department and a large geriatric unit. Therefore, in my opinion, they definitely needed a speech therapist. However, there was no room available. I persuaded him to have a good look around the hospital and off we went. Eventually we found accommodation that was ultimately going to be demolished but in the meantime was sitting there not being used. And so a speech therapy department was set up in the City Hospital.

In September that year, three students who were on our bursary scheme had graduated. Now I had three new staff to provide services.

Six months after that I was at a conference in Cardiff and I met a speech therapist who had originally come from Northern Ireland. During the course of the conference I enquired if she would like to return to the Province and I offered her any kind of post she liked. She eventually said if I could offer her a post with children with a physical disability she would be interested. Of course I was delighted, because I had two schools which would suit this role. Not long after that she came to Belfast, visited the schools and a few days later not only did she phone and say she would take the post, but also to say she had a friend Marie who would like to come to Belfast as well. It's hard to believe that all I did at that time was ring the personnel department, say I had two more speech therapists and they were appointed – no interviews, references anything.

I contacted Marie and asked her if, before she started her new school post, she would be willing to run a six week course of intensive therapy for teenage boys. She was delighted.

I will now relate what happened to the boy with the stammer and severe speech and language defect whom I saw in the country. I contacted staff in the local community clinics and ended up with five teenage boys, and the boy (Dominic) from the country made the sixth. Now the problem was how to get Dominic to Belfast every morning for six weeks. To solve this problem I contacted the local churches to enquire if anyone would be willing to give him a lift to Belfast. It was no problem at all! We eventually found someone very suitable. Luckily we were able to use the rooms we had just acquired in the City Hospital. The boys attended every day from approximately 9.30 a.m. to 3.30 p.m. for therapy. At lunchtime they usually left the clinic and went on trips to the Botanic Gardens or the Museum. A very sad comment made by one of these boys made me realise what a restricted life some of them were leading. On one of their trips they were going up a local tree-lined avenue and one boy asked the therapist:

"Hey Miss, is this a forest?"

I often wonder if this comment made me, a few years later, set up our intensive therapy and holiday-scheme for our children.

The boys all improved considerably. Dominic's speech improved, his stammer was almost gone and he returned to school. Intensive therapy worked again.

For the next number of years I did battle with every District to get rooms for staff, even in new facilities where there was a therapist on the revenue consequences, sometimes no accommodation was provided. In one new health centre the only room we were offered was a locker room that was to be used by a porter. In a new geriatric unit I went to see where our room was. To my amazement when I opened the door I saw a chiropody chair. The first half of the room had lino on the floor, the other side had carpet. There was a curtain to divide the two halves of the room. So one half was for a speech therapist to work, and the other half was for a chiropodist. It

62

became known as the 'foot and mouth room'. It was rejected by both the area chiropodist and by me. We did manage to acquire more suitable accommodation.

In 1975 a speech therapy training course was set up in Jordanstown Polytechnic. Earlier that year the four Area Therapists were asked if they would participate in the interviews with the newly appointed Courses Director, Mary Thomas.

We were not as inundated with applications that year as we were to be a number of years later. Speech therapy at that time was not particularly good from either a salary or a career point of view. Just to give you an example, my starting salary as the Area Speech Therapist for the Eastern Board was £1600 per year. Prior to 1974 there were only two grades i.e. speech therapist or senior speech therapist and the only way you could become a senior speech therapist was to have two speech therapists working for you. And for many years in Northern Ireland this was impossible as there were so few staff.

The first intake to Jordanstown was to be ten students. Eastern Board that year provided bursaries for five of these students.

The four Area Therapists continued to participate in the interviews for the Polytechnic for many years after that. As salary and grading structure improved, we sometimes had a bus full of applicants coming from different schools across the Province and from the Republic.

In 1976 another event was to take place which had a major influence on my life. I received a letter from a therapist in England saying that there was a proposal to set up an Association of Area Speech Therapists, as this type of management responsibility had not been undertaken on such a scale before. I was invited to attend the inaugural meeting to check out the feasibility of this proposal. I talked this over with the other Area Therapists and I was asked to go to represent Northern Ireland.

On the morning I arrived there must have been fifty or sixty therapists there, I think I only knew one of them. By chance I ended up sitting beside someone who was to become a very close friend of mine. Her name was Lena Rustin. Lena was a real character! She was, as they would say in Belfast, 'five-foot nothing', very slim, always wore very high heels and designer clothes. She was an expert on stammering and lectured on it across the world.

Following coffee there was general discussion on whether to start such an association and a vote was taken as to whether a steering committee should be set up. That was agreed. Nominations were then called for and written on the board. As the nominations went up, it was obvious that everybody nominated and seconded was from London. So I got up and gave my name and said that I came from Northern Ireland. I said I felt there should be more of a regional representation on the committee. As I did not know anyone there I proposed that there should be someone from Scotland or the North of Ireland on the committee. That day there was no one there from Scotland. So, a few minutes later someone got up and proposed me. And, to my surprise, when the votes were counted I was on the steering committee! This involved me in a number of meetings in London. When the next meeting of Area Speech Therapists was held we presented the constitution that we had drawn up. It was accepted. It was proposed and seconded that the current steering committee should become the first committee of what was to be TASTM (The Association of Area Speech Therapist Managers).

I remained as the representative for Northern Ireland until I left the health service. One of the great advantages of being on this committee and part of the Association was that I was able to hear of any new tests or new methods of treatment. As I was always very interested in providing training for my staff, I was able to arrange for some of these therapists to come to Northern Ireland to provide the courses. Lena Rustin, whom I met for the first time at Bedford, came many times. As I said, she specialised in stammering and came to do the Monteray Fluency Course and a Behavioural Interview one for us. Those who attended that particular course will probably never forget it!

Lena was quite a character. One time she came to stay with me and of course, not realising she was Jewish I gave her an Ulster fry for breakfast. Luckily for me she didn't, as she said, 'keep a Jewish house'. For years after, every time we met she would shout:

"Hello Eleanor, what about me tattie bread?!" in a very strong Cockney accent. She really was a great character.

9

Post 1974: A very busy time

The years following my appointment as Area Speech Therapist became increasingly busy. Although my clinical work was cut down in my usual community clinic, I began to take on work in clinics outside Belfast.

The first one was following a meeting I was asked to attend with the Association of Primary Headmasters from South-East Education and Library Board. The Eastern Health and Social Service Board contained two Education and Library Boards. At that meeting I was made aware of the urgent need for speech therapy in what was originally County Down. One headmaster in particular stressed the serious problems he was having in his school, so I said I would go down and assess the situation. I arranged to go down the following week and asked him to have a list of children who the teachers thought needed therapy.

The following Friday morning I went down to the school which consisted of four hundred boys aged four to eleven. The initial list I was given had ninety-three names which I eventually discovered did not cover all the boys in the school with speech defects. That meant that over twenty-five percent of the children needed treatment. Every Friday morning after that I went down to the school. The problem in the area was that there had been no speech therapist for some time. Many of these children, if there had been a therapist, would have been seen, assessed and started having treatment before commencing their education. I have to pay tribute here to the teachers of this school, who really did work with me to provide help for the children. In addition there was one classroom assistant who sat in on Friday mornings to observe the work when I was there. She was given leave to go over the lessons with some of the children during the week.

I went there every Friday morning until, I think, 1979 when the first students graduated from Jordanstown Polytechnic and I was able to provide a speech therapist for the District.

These years became increasingly busy as there was the involvement with the new course at Jordanstown Polytechnic, I had my involvement with the Association of Speech Therapy Managers and I myself was involved in doing management training courses, for example – selection and interviewing, first-line management, middle management, etc.

I don't remember when bursaries started being provided for students wanting to take up speech therapy; I think this was probably in the late 1950s. At that time speech therapy was not a degree course. It was a three-year course and students qualifying were awarded an L.C.S.T. (Licentiate of the College of Speech Therapists). All courses were either in England or in Scotland, and because it was not a university course, students had to get a discretionary award rather than a scholarship. This discretionary award covered tuition fees and very little else. Therefore parents had to be willing to pay a considerable amount of money each year to support their children. Once bursaries started to be paid, many more pupils started to be interested in training. Degree courses were started in some places from 1970, which improved the situation. From 1974 onwards I arranged for students on bursaries to come to see me during their holidays. This had the advantage of letting them meet their future colleagues; it also allowed them to discuss with me any problems they may have been having with their training. Occasionally I would arrange for them to have additional help if they were having difficulty with a particular subject. When newly qualified therapists were appointed I also arranged for them to see me once a month on a Monday morning (their admin morning). We would visit different clinics throughout the area and again offer support regarding problems they could be having. It must be remembered that at that time there were no experienced therapists in all of the Districts. Some children with severe problems did pose difficulties for newly qualified staff. Again I told them that I would be willing to come any time they wanted me to see a patient for them.

On a personal note, during this time my son went to study English at a University in Scotland in 1975 and my daughter went to study medicine at Queen's University Belfast two years later. In 1977 I was asked if I would consider being captain of my golf club, so that year I was vice-captain and in 1978 I was captain. As I had not played any golf in the years 1974 to 1976 my handicap had lapsed but in 1977 I was playing again and my handicap went up to 13. Unfortunately my handicap lapsed again in my captain's year as I didn't have time to play golf. In July 1979 I remarried. Jack Gildea was a widower with a seven-year-old son Andrew who became my second son.

As I mentioned, those years were very busy!

10

Case Stories

The majority of children attending school clinics probably do so because they have a speech and/or language disorder. This type of disorder is more common in boys than in girls. The only speech defect that is more common in girls is a 'lisp'. This is because it is, or was, considered to be very 'thweet' if a little girl lisps. As this book is not intended primarily for therapists I won't go into all of the reasons why someone would have this type of disorder except to say that it is not, as once thought, due to a tongue tie. This does happen but it is rare. The disorder can be due to hearing problems, lack of stimulation, family history of speech problems, etc. The articulation problem can be as simple as a child being unable to make a few sounds, for example saying a 't' sound instead of a 'k' sound i.e. saying 'tar' instead of 'car', or 'poon' instead of 'spoon', or 'tool' instead of 'school'. In the worst cases all sounds are affected and speech is unintelligible. With the language disorder it can go from the child being slow to use words, to not being able to talk at all. In the worst cases of language disorders, children may be referred to a language unit which is usually attached to a school.

Betty was referred to me when she was five years old. She had a severe articulation problem, her speech was almost unintelligible and her language was slightly delayed. I explained to her mother that we would be seeing her once a week. Mrs Smith attended with Betty for probably two to three weeks and then stopped. The usual procedure was to wait for a couple of weeks in case the child or parent had been ill and then send another appointment. Two further appointments were sent, neither was kept and Betty was discharged. About two years after that the headmaster of her school phoned me to ask why she wasn't having any therapy and I explained what had happened. He said that he would speak to her mother and asked me to send another appointment. The same thing happened as before. After two weeks Betty did not come back. Another two years passed. Again the headmaster phoned me. This time I insisted that the mother would attend with Betty to see if I could understand why the child would not attend for treatment. Mrs Smith did attend and what she said was:

"I don't understand why everybody is getting in such a fuss about Betty's speech, she sounds alright to me."

I then made a recording to let Mrs Smith hear Betty talking. When I played the recording back she said:

"Who's that?"

"That is Betty," I replied, but she did not believe me. I then asked her to read a sentence and then asked Betty to read one and we alternated that for a few minutes. I then played it back. And at last Mrs Smith believed what she was hearing.

I don't think I ever saw Mrs Smith again, but Betty attended very regularly. She was a lovely little girl and we got on very well together. She was a little plump (like me) and occasionally her mother would send a small box of chocolates. Betty would give the chocolates to me and then say:

"You don't want to eat all of them or else you'll get fat!"

I would then open the chocolates and Betty would tuck in!

When her speech and language were normal and it was time for me to discharge her, she did not want to go, so she continued to call in occasionally to see me. She is now married with two children of her own. When I started treating her it was about thirty years ago and I still get a Christmas card with a long letter in it every year. Occasionally she will write, "Don't eat too much or you will get fat!"

One morning I was in the clinic and my secretary phoned through to say that there was a woman with a young child asking to see me. The woman appeared quite distraught. I told my secretary I would see the woman after I had finished treating the patient I was with at that time. About fifteen or twenty minutes later Mrs Foster came in with her little boy of about four years old, called Gordon. The story was as follows: Gordon could not talk at all, he just made a series of grunting noises such as 'ugh, ugh', and used gesture to communicate. For example when he wanted to go out on his bicycle he would make circular motions with his arms, trying to imitate the wheels on his bicycle and follow this with another, 'ugh, ugh'. Mrs Foster, who I found to be a very conscientious and caring mother, had gone to see every GP in their practice and as usual what happened in those days was told:

"He will grow out of it."

Thirty or forty years ago people did not know very much about speech therapy and GPs had received no training on it. When I started working full-time, one of the services I did was to provide training for the GPs.

71

That morning when Mrs Foster came home from seeing the GP she happened to meet a neighbour. Gordon was pulling at his mother's skirt and doing his normal 'ugh, ugh' and the neighbour asked:

"Does he always speak like that?"

Mrs Foster got quite defensive about this comment and explained that she had been to see the doctor and had been told that Gordon would grow out of it. The neighbour said:

"Don't you listen to that. You take him up now to see Mrs Shaw at the clinic. My wee boy couldn't talk and I took him there, she fixed him."

Hence Mrs Foster was with me that morning. I checked Gordon and found that he had a tongue-tie. This is not as common as some people think. I referred him to the dental hospital to have it cut. Dentists will cut it on the grounds of dental hygiene. Just think how often you use your tongue to clean your teeth.

Once the operation was done, Gordon was taken on for treatment and very soon was speaking normally. Mrs Foster became my greatest fan, every time she met someone she would say:

"If it hadn't of been for Mrs Shaw, my Gordon wouldn't have been talking!"

One morning when she had arrived with Gordon for treatment she asked if I would mind if she didn't stay as she had a message to do. I said this was quite alright. She then said if he needed to go to the toilet would someone take him and again I said yes that was fine. She then mentioned that she thought, to quote:

"I think there is something wrong with him down there."

So I told her I would take him to see the clinical medical officer. While Mrs Foster was on her message I took Gordon up to see the doctor who discovered he had an undescended testicle and Gordon was referred up to the hospital. So after that Mrs Foster would go around saying:

"If it hadn't of been for Mrs Shaw we wouldn't have known about Gordon's tongue-tie and his undescended testicle!"

A few months prior to this, I had been examining students and noticed that very many of them did not tick the boxes on the case history sheet relating to condition of tongue, teeth, palate, lips, etc. I was quite sure that the students had checked the condition but simply had not entered on the case file. So at a staff meeting, I had said to the staff that in order to set a good example for the students, they too should record that this had been done. At a later staff meeting one of the therapists got up and amid some laughter, enquired how I had discovered Gordon's undescended testicle.

I replied, "Well, as I told you before, when seeing a patient it is important to do a thorough examination!"

I never told them that it was Mrs Foster herself who had discovered it!

About ten years ago, that is about thirty years following the events above, I was with my husband when he was attending a cardiac out-patient department and who was there, but Mrs Foster. She came over to speak to me and I introduced her to my husband. You've probably guessed it; the first thing she said was:

"If it hadn't been for Mrs Shaw…"

She included the story of the undescended testicle!

When parents came to the clinic after receiving an appointment sometimes they wondered, like Mrs Smith, why they had been sent an appointment as they themselves did not perceive there to be any problem with the child's speech. Sometimes, like Mrs Foster, they were delighted that someone was finally taking an interest in a problem they were acutely aware of. However, I did have one case which was bizarre, the mother only wanted me to correct one word which the child could not say correctly, despite the fact that the child said very little. Unfortunately the child loved fish fingers, the trouble was, the only thing he was able to say was fish, except that he pronounced it as 'pish'. As soon as he went into a shop, he would shout 'Pish! pish!' at the top of his voice.

I ended up successfully treating this boy, much to the mother's delight.

Counselling very often played a part when we were treating children with articulation problems. Mr White attended the clinic with his son Paul. Paul was an only child and was very spoilt. Mr White would relate stories to me when he would come to the clinic with Paul regarding his behaviour. For example he told me that one morning Corn Flakes had fallen on the floor and were lying there when Paul got down from the table. Paul walked on them and found they made a crunching noise. So every morning from then on Paul would deliberately throw Corn Flakes on the floor. I did try talking to Mr White when he was relating these stories encouraging him not to spoil his son, but he thought they were very funny.

One day he came in and told me how the previous evening Paul wanted to play with the clock on the mantelpiece. Of course Mr White lifted the clock down and gave it to him to play with! So Paul sat on the floor, pulled off the door, pulled off the hands and ended up with the clock in pieces. I found this incredible that a parent would let his child do such a thing. So I said to Mr White:

"Mr White, do you think this is a good thing to spoil your child like this? Children must learn what is acceptable to do and what is not. He should be told that he cannot ask for a clock to be handed down and then pull it apart."

I was well into my theme of how children should be treated when Mr White suddenly leaned over the desk and said:

"Mrs Shaw."

I paused and waited. I thought he was going to say something like: "You're quite right, my wife and I have been spoiling Paul. We must be more responsible in how we treat him."

Instead he said:

"Mrs Shaw, you have lovely teeth...are they all your own?"

Another incident involved the mother of a patient. I greatly admired this woman. She used to come to the clinic with three little boys who all had problems with their tonsils and adenoids and all had seriously runny noses. It was the eldest child that I was treating and during the time she attended, the mother told me how she really longed for a daughter, but as she had had three caesarean sections it was not advisable to have another pregnancy. So she had put her name down to adopt a girl. One day she came in she told me that she had an appointment the next week to see a child that might be suitable. A few weeks later she returned to the clinic. She told me that when she had gone to the hostel to see the little girl, she was a coloured child. At that time in Northern Ireland, it was uncommon to see anyone who was non-Caucasian. Due to the severe unemployment in Northern Ireland there was a government policy that work had to be offered to a resident of the country first. So apart from students at the universities we didn't have any immigrants here. While Mrs Allen would have been delighted to take the child, she and her husband decided after a great deal of heart-searching, that it might not be good to bring this child into their area as she could be bullied or teased.

I didn't see Mrs Allen for a few months after this and when I saw her again she came in with this two-year-old boy who had, could you believe it, a seriously runny nose! What had happened was she had gone up again to the hostel to see if there were any other girls and the person in charge said:

"No there are no children at all for adoption at this time except one. A little boy, nearly two years old and nobody wants to adopt him."

So she went and looked and there this little boy just sitting there. She thought, *Well, I've got three of them already all with runny noses, one more won't hurt!*

She said:

"I think God didn't mean me to have a little girl, just boys with runny noses!"

That child got a very loving home.

The clinic I worked in was a school health clinic, so we did not see anyone after they left school at eighteen. However, one day a woman named Mrs Murray came in. She had previously attended the clinic with her two sons. However, I had not been treating them, it was another therapist. Mrs Murray had called up to the clinic and asked to see me. She had quite a severe speech defect and having seen a programme on television had contacted the College of Speech Therapists to ask where she should go for treatment. They had given her my name. I wasn't sure whether I could do anything for her speech defect at that stage. She was just over fifty years of age. Firstly I did not know whether she would be able to change at that age. Secondly, I wasn't sure if I would be allowed to treat her at the clinic. I thought I could get round that difficulty, so I discussed with her why she wanted treatment at this age in life. Eventually we decided that she would attend for a trial period to see how she got on. She did attend for I think about six or eight months and her speech did improve. There were certain sounds we didn't attempt to correct, for example the 'r' and 'th' sounds. These are always late sounds to develop. After all we do have a number of TV personalities who are also unable to make 'r' sounds! We were both very pleased with the progress she made. I saw her periodically after that. She continued to practise at home with a tape recorder.

During the years when I was working mainly in a clinical role I would become very frustrated when children that I knew I could help were not brought for treatment by their parents. One of the families I remember particularly was the Larmours. There were two little boys aged about three and five. On the morning they came for their initial appointment they were brought in by what looked like a sixteen-year-old girl. She was very slim, pale and had thin blonde hair. She looked about sixteen, but she was, in fact, their mother. The two children had dark hair. The front part looked as if it had been 'licked' down and the back was quite bushy and looked as if it had jam and other bits of food in it. They had a very bad smell. Both children had quite severe articulation problems and I queried their language as well.

About a week previously we had attended a course on how to administer the Reynell Test which looked at children's comprehension and expressive language abilities. We had been advised that for the first few times we administered the test there should be two therapists involved, one to administer the test and one to score it. So following the visit by the Larmours I arranged for a colleague to come over to do the test with me. I advised my colleague not to sit too close to the children. However, she must have forgotten what I said, because as the test progressed she started looking quite queasy.

Following the test I arranged with Mrs Larmour to bring the children for treatment and you've guessed it, they didn't turn up! There was no response to a further appointment and then I discovered that the family had moved house. Another appointment was sent to the new address, the family turned up for treatment and a few weeks later vanished once more. They had, again, moved house. When I eventually discovered where they had gone, I paid a home visit. It was impossible to believe the squalor they were living in. The place was filthy; there was a large dog bounding about, a huge fire in the grate and a very large television. Mrs Larmour said that they were now very well settled in this house and they would definitely keep future appointments. However, away they went again! I don't remember how they finished up; I think they just seemed to be people who permanently moved. We eventually lost track of them. They were two lovely boys who were probably in a loving, caring family that couldn't cope.

When I first went to work in the community clinic in the country I was only seeing children. I had worked with adult patients when I was in the hospital, but my work in Belfast School Health Services was exclusively with children. In the early '70s, when asked to be an examiner for the Dublin College, I obviously had to have an up-to-date knowledge of work with patients with aphasia, so some revision on the subject was necessary. However, I had not actually treated a patient for a number of years. One morning when I was at the clinic one of the health visitors asked me if I would see a stroke patient called Bernie. On assessment all she could say was 'dootin, dootin, dootin'. Her husband Paddy had a heart problem and as there were steps into the clinic it was difficult for him to get his wife out of the wheelchair and carry her in, so I suggested treatment would be better at their home, a few miles outside of the town.

The following week Paddy arrived to show me the way to their home. So, off we went, Paddy in his car in front and me following. I don't think he knew there was anything called a speed limit! He went through the town and out to the country probably at about seventy miles an hour! Eventually we turned off the main road and I, not knowing the way, had to slow down. I watched him vanish in the distance. After about a mile or so he realised I wasn't behind him any more and waited for me to catch up.

They lived in a large farmhouse in the most beautiful spot in the country surrounded by mountains. When I came in, Bernie was sitting in a chair by a roaring fire. I gathered that she actually spent most of her time just sitting there. They were a delightful couple to visit.

A few weeks later I spoke to one of my senior staff and asked her if she would come with me. I wanted to make sure that I wasn't missing anything and to see if there was any other treatment that I could provide. So at eight o'clock one morning the following week Jane and I set off to see Bernie. When we arrived she was still in bed. We went in to the bedroom, Jane assessed her and following that assured me that I was on the right lines for treatment. When we came back into the main room, Paddy had set the table. At that time in the country you knew you were accepted when the food came out for you. There on the table was some cooked ham, some tomatoes, bread, cake, jam, etc. I could feel Jane stiffening beside me as she was very diet conscious and I whispered out the side of my mouth, "You eat that! I don't want to offend Paddy!"

And she did. They were a lovely couple, very happy together. Each week when I came Bernie would say, 'dootin, dootin, dootin' waving her good arm and Paddy would interpret:

"She wants to know how your son is?" he would say. Or:

"She wants to know if you've got any holidays planned?" Or:

"She's asking how your mother is?"

And she would nod and smile and I would tell them all about the family. I remember one day asking Paddy if they had any family themselves, and he just laughed and said:

"No, she was too auld!"

Every day when I was leaving he was always trying to persuade me to have 'a wee scotch!' I had to explain to him that it was more than my job was worth turning up to the clinic in the afternoon smelling of alcohol. However, I did promise that if I was ever down for a visit to that part of the country at a weekend I would call in. And one Sunday with my husband and mother we were down in that area and we called in to see them. They were delighted. I was glad I had never agreed to have 'a wee scotch' – Paddy did not know the meaning of 'wee'!

A few months later when I returned from a holiday Mary, the caretaker at the clinic, told me that Bernie had died very suddenly when I was away. So after the clinic that morning I drove out to see Paddy. When he heard the car he came out and he was crying. He came over, gave me a big hug, and said:

"I knew you would come when you heard my Bernie was dead."

Paddy died not long afterwards. As I said, they were a lovely couple and I missed visiting them.

One morning a woman arrived in the clinic with a toddler and a baby. The toddler, aged about four or five, had a speech problem. I talked this over with the mother and during the course of our discussion she began to tell me about her married life.

She wasn't particularly happy at that moment in time; her husband had lost his job, making it difficult to support the family. She told me that prior to the arrival of the younger child, she and her husband had been very happy and their sex life was thoroughly enjoyable. Since losing his job, he had started to go to the snooker club every night with his friends and would normally not return home until midnight. By that time she was tired and relations were not particularly good for her.

We talked over all problems. I felt that the time was not right for her to attend the clinic each week. I reassured her about her son's speech and said I would see her again in a few months' time.

About four months later I sent for her again. I asked her if she was feeling any happier and she told me the situation at home was terrible. One day she'd realised that her husband coming home at midnight every night meant they really had no life together any more. She had been reading magazines and an article in one said that sometimes after having a baby, a woman may not look after herself as she should and her husband may lose interest in her.

So, she said, she had gone down to the market and bought herself a lovely black nightdress. She came home and that evening, after tidying up and sending the children to bed she spent some time putting on her make-up and new black nightdress. She lay on the sofa waiting for her husband to arrive. At midnight the door opened, her husband came in and he took one look at her before saying, "Oh my God," and then he ran off. She said she hadn't seen him since.

Following that she had spoken to his friends. It turned out that instead of going to the snooker club he had actually been seeing his girlfriend on the other side of town. I commiserated with her and spent time discussing her present situation. There was nothing else I could do and she left. Just a few weeks prior to this my husband had died. I hadn't mentioned this to any of the clients, but shortly after she left that morning there was a knock on my door. She came back in and told me, "I'm very sorry, I have just heard that your husband died. Here I am talking about my sex life and how much I miss it," she patted my hand and said, "but you really do miss it, don't you?"

Mrs Hobson was a lovely little lady. She was a very good mother and never missed an appointment with her children, one of her habits was anytime she told you anything about one of her children, she would emphasise the point by pushing that child on the shoulder and say 'isn't that right?' She would always arrive at the clinic in her carpet slippers and often would tell us that she just had 'a wee perm'. This meant that she had been to the hairdresser; her hair had been cut quite short and then had been very tightly permed.

One day she was telling us about when the children had their tea at night, it went something like this:

"See, every night when I'm giving them their tea I don't get time to get the jam on the bread before they've grabbed the piece and ate it."

At this point she would give the nearest child a light thump on the shoulder to get their attention.

"Isn't that right?" she would say to them after their thump.

Another day she came into the therapist and said to her son:

"Sammy." *Thump* "Tell the woman what your mummy bought you for your iced lollies."

Another thump

"A fridge, Miss."

The funniest story I think regarding Mrs Hobson was when I heard her talking to someone outside my room. One of her children was attending an assessment unit and she really wanted all her children to go there. This is roughly what I heard:

"See our Hughie – Our wee Hughie goes to that school up the road, it's just great. See since our Hughie went there, he has become very polite, he says 'memmy and deddy'. See our Sammy..."

Sammy got another thump.

"He says 'hey ma, hey da'."

Thump again

"Don't you Sammy, isn't that right?"

So many of the mothers we had were wonderful and caring people like Mrs Hobson.

Occasionally we did get the other type of parent who really didn't care. I remember a young teenager who was referred to me; she had quite a severe speech defect, but had not received any treatment because the mother had not kept any appointments when she was younger. The girl came for an assessment and I felt that despite the problems with her speech she seemed quite an intelligent child. It was confirmed by the educational psychologist that she would have an IQ of 120. Unfortunately I got no support from the mother. The girl, who would have been able to attend by herself was often kept home from school to do messages for her mother or just be there for company. I tried talking to the mother but to no avail. She had a number of children and they were all neglected. I remember going to our clinical medical officer one morning, I was very angry. The girl had not attended for treatment again. I remember saying to Dr. Campbell, "I think that parents who do not send their children for treatment should not receive child benefit."

Dr. Campbell did not think that legislation would ever be approved.

One of the children I remember very well was called Johnny. He attended me for a slight speech defect. He really was a lovely child to treat. One day when he came in, there was a birthday card on my desk. As it was his birthday the next day, I was joking with him that if he had been born a day earlier we could have been twins. I then asked him what age he was going to be the next day and he said, "I'll be five."

So I asked him, "What age do you think I am today?"

He studied me very closely and then said, "A hundred." Any time I met his parents after that they always reminded me of this story and we still laughed.

In those days you treated children and indeed adults, until you thought their speech was age appropriate, before they were put on review.

A recent poll relating to the economic situation showed that many people felt that savings could be made by cutting down on the number of speech therapists. I wonder if the people who made this suggestion and who were quite articulate realised one day in the future they may need a speech therapist. They may have a stroke, a head injury following a car accident etc, or they may have a neurological condition, multiple sclerosis, Parkinson's disease, cancer etc. Relating to stroke, many people find that following a stroke they are unable to understand what is said to them, they themselves cannot talk, they cannot read nor can they write. Can you imagine what it would be like to wake up in hospital and find yourself in that situation? It would be almost like you being transported to China.

You could hear the people, you could see the people and you could see the written word but you would not be able to understand anything. This happens to many thousands of people every year at any age.

Stammering is probably the one speech defect that most people know about. In fact it was the first speech problem to be recognised and a service to treat stammers was set up in Manchester hospital in the 1930s.

When a mother comes to the clinic with a child with a stammer the first question that is asked is, "When did the stammer start?" If the answer is the child has always stammered then what the therapist would usually do is an assessment of the child's speech and language. The reason for this is if you find that there is a discrepancy between the child's comprehension and his or her expressive ability then that can be the reason for the stammer. If you think about learning a foreign language, say French for example, you go to France on holiday and want to ask how you can get to the railway station. You may be able to say, 'can you tell me' in French, but you can't remember the word of 'the way' so you will hesitate and perhaps say 'ehhhhhh' and change it to the road and then you don't know the word for the station so you may change it to 'where the train goes?' So children who have a difficulty with language may stammer as they search for the word. The therapist will start that child on a language programme. In some cases a referral might also be made to an educational psychologist for an intelligence test.

More commonly the mother will tell you the child spoke perfectly well until a certain incident, for example, he may have had to go into hospital, there may be a new baby in the family or he was frightened by a dog etc. You then enquire whether there is anyone in the family who has stammered and they will often say 'yes'. These are the 'two ps' we were taught in college, the predisposition and precipitating factors. The unfortunate thing is that when a child starts to stammer, what usually happens is the parents or grandparents or other people correct him or her and say 'don't do that' or 'stop that' or 'say it again' or 'take a deep breath' or some alternative. Unfortunately because children cannot stop doing it, they just become more and more conscious of the stammer and so it continues. When treating older patients, what they often tell you is that they feel guilty when they stammer because they feel they are doing something they shouldn't do.

I have thought about this a lot and wonder if it is because we do not find out the reason it continues. We can do all the usual work e.g. shadow reading, discussing home and/or school life, but the stammer continues. Research is currently going on looking at the brains of people who have stammered. However I'm not sure if this is the problem area. So often a stammer that has proven resistant to treatment will cease if the person's circumstances change.

I remember one boy I treated, a teenager. He came from a good working class family and was an average student. He didn't appear to have any worries about school or home life. I tried every known treatment. His parents did not draw attention to his speech but he still stammered. He left school and many years later I met him again. He was working in a shop – no sign of a stammer but it was very obvious he was homosexual. People nowadays don't think much of this but forty years ago it was still illegal and if someone was caught in a homosexual relationship they could be imprisoned. I often wonder if that was the reason for his stammer.

When I first went to work in a community clinic and met with the health visitors, I asked them what they did during the medical inspection when they found a child who had a stammer. The reply was that the child would be reviewed the next year. I told them that in future, when they found a child with a stammer they were to refer them to me immediately. The parents and family of children with a stammer must be advised as soon as possible that they are not, under any circumstances, to draw attention to it. However, getting some parents to stop correcting the child is difficult.

One morning at the clinic I saw a mother with a 14-year-old boy, and I asked her what happened when he stammered, her reply was:

"Well it really annoys me, so I tell him to stop it and say it again."

So I advised her and explained to her why she shouldn't correct him and said I would review him in a few months to see if this brought any improvement. A few months later, when I saw him again, the stammer was just as bad and the mother said:

"Look love, it really irritates me when he does that. I just get so annoyed that I keep telling him to stop it."

So I arranged for him to start treatment in a few weeks' time. However, when I sent for him I received a phone call to say that his mother could not bring him as an older daughter was pregnant and as there were some complications, she was going over to England to stay with her. Therapy was postponed until the mother returned. The pregnancy and birth were complicated. The mother didn't return from England for a number of months. When the boy was seen again, the stammer was almost non-existent and his mother said:

"Look love, I'll tell you if I had still been at home he would still be stammering, because I know I would have continued shouting at him. But my other daughter was looking after the house and she didn't have time and didn't bother. So you were quite right."

It's a sad fact that despite the advice many parents still continue to ignore it.

Robert came to me when he was a teenager. He was a very good looking, intelligent young boy, but his stammer was quite bad. From the case history, I learned that his father who also had a stammer had married late in life and Robert was his only child. Naturally he wanted his son to do well at school and excel in sport etc. He certainly didn't want him to have a stammer! As usual at the interview I explained to his mother the importance of not drawing attention to the stammer and while I think Robert's mother carried out my advice, the father did not. Each week when Robert attended I would hear that his father was still correcting him. I gathered that considerable pressure was being put on Robert regarding his school work. This was, in fact, having the opposite effect to what his father wanted. I decided that I would ask if his father would attend the clinic one day with his wife and I would talk to both of them. For the first time in my years of practice, I lost patience with a parent. From the beginning of the interview Robert's father just kept on making comments such as, 'He's a yyyyyoung mmman now, he shshshould stop stammering', 'He should pppull himself together', 'His grades are not good enough.' The main theme of his argument was at Robert's age he should know better than to stammer. So I said, "Mr Gordon, you are considerably older than Robert. You have stammered since you came in to see me this afternoon. Do you not think at your age *you* should pull *yourself* together and stop stammering?" I would like to report that my talk did some good. It didn't! Robert left school at age eighteen. He left home very soon after that. He never fulfilled his full potential, and he didn't go to university as he had planned. I did meet him many years later. He no longer lived here, the stammer had gone and he was doing very, very well in his chosen career. It's a very sad thing that some parents who are ambitious for their children put too much pressure on them. It's as if having a stammer makes their child less than perfect.

On a lighter note, Tommy was a young boy who was attending for treatment. He came from a very large family and when he came in each week I would ask him how he was getting on at school and how things were at home. It was a very happy family, but as in all families, Tommy was constantly being teased. One day he came in and I asked him how he had been talking that week, and he replied:

"I have been stammering very badly."

"And why was that?" I asked.

"Because our Billy was annoying me," he replied.

"What was he doing to annoy you this week?"

"He was calling me names."

"What was he calling you?"

"He was calling me Yogi Bear."

I wasn't sure how to reply to this, so I asked:

"What's wrong with that? You watch Yogi Bear on television and you like him."

"Well, I don't like it when he calls me Yogi Bear."

"And what do you do then?"

"I call him names," he replied. "I call him ban the bomb."

I walked straight into it.

"Why do you call him that?"

And he replied, "Because he farts all night! One night I counted and he farted twenty-three times!"

Thank goodness there was a filing cabinet behind me and I could turn around to hide my laughter!

I first saw Graham before he started school. He was about four and a half years of age, but was a very tall child, he looked about seven! Both his mother and father were also very tall. From taking the case history, I thought that what was happening was that because Graham looked about seven years old he was being treated as a seven-year-old. I asked the mother to remember that he was actually only four and a half, and as usual advised not to draw attention to the stammer.

I saw Graham again just before he started school and the mother reported that the stammer had almost gone. She and her husband were delighted. I advised her that I would see Graham again in six months' time, but I emphasised as usual that if the stammer returned in the meantime she was to phone me immediately.

A few months later she did contact me to say that Graham was stammering again. I arranged to see him. His mother could not tell me anything that had happened to upset him, so I brought Graham in and endeavoured to find out something that could have brought the stammer back. Eventually I asked him what he liked doing when he came home from school, and he said:

"I like reading."

"What are you reading now?" I asked.

"*The Wind in the Willows.*"

As it happened, I was reading the same book to my children at that time and thought that it would have been impossible for Graham to read such a story. So I asked:

"Is Mummy reading the book to you?"

"No," he replied.

So I said, "Has it got lots of pictures in it?"

"Emm, no," he said.

Now, I could not believe that Graham was reading the *Wind in the Willows* at his age so I brought over some books for him to read. And, you've guessed it; he was able to read all of them. And more importantly, read with understanding. So here I had a child, not yet five, able to read advanced books and at school he was reading 'Here is Dick, Here is Dora'. He was bored at school! I talked to his mother and arranged for Graham to be referred to the educational psychologist. It turned out he had a very high IQ. Unfortunately, while our educational system allows for specialist schooling for children with very low IQs, it offers little help for children at the other end of the spectrum.

Graham was moved up a class at school, so for the next years he was studying with children at least a year older than he was. Socially, this was difficult for him as he was still only a little boy, but mentally he was well in advance of the rest of the class. We were able to provide advice to the parents on how to deal with this and the stammer did improve. However, Graham did not realise his full potential until he was in his twenties. When last I heard about him, he was doing very well indeed.

Counselling was such a part of my treatment with children and adults who stammered. However, as I haven't worked as a clinician for many years now, I wonder how therapists are able to do this with the restricted time that they now have with patients, no wonder waiting lists are growing.

Jamie was the youngest of a family of five, he had four older sisters. His father was absolutely delighted when Jamie was born, a boy at last! The problem, as I gathered over some time working with Jamie, was that he was seriously overprotected. He was hardly ever allowed out before he started school and never allowed to play any 'rough-and-tumble' games, so when he went to school he just stood in the playground and didn't join in. The trouble was the other boys made fun of him and he definitely got bullied. So, my aim was to try and help this. I was not able to see the father as he was working, so I explained to his mother that I would like his father to play with Jamie a bit more and be a bit more 'rough' with him. At home I had a punch-ball that my own son had used. I brought it down to the clinic and Jamie practised hitting it. I also encouraged him to walk along a bench and jump off. This progressed to jumping off a chair; initially he held my hand but eventually managed on his own. I think he even jumped off a desk. I am glad the health and safety people weren't around in those days or I think Jamie would still be stammering! At home his father also started playing football with him. Before treatment began his mother could not let him out to play in the street as he invariably came back in crying, saying that somebody had hit him or pushed him. I felt that treatment was definitely working when his mother came in one day to tell me that a neighbour had called to complain that Jamie had pushed her son. I reassured the mother that, in my opinion, Jamie was not an aggressive child and she need not to worry. Jamie began to play out in the street and joined in with the other kids in the playground at school, his stammer cleared up in no time.

I decided one time that we should try taking a group of teenage stammerers for intensive therapy. I contacted an outdoor pursuit centre located in the Mourne Mountains and arranged for the five boys to stay for a week at the hostel. The boys would have therapy every morning and would then be taken out in the afternoons by a trained instructor who had organised activities for them. So off the two therapists went with the boys.

One afternoon trip consisted of canoeing on the lake. This was slightly difficult for one of the therapists who was, shall we say, a little on the plump side! However, she squeezed herself in to the canoe and said she would definitely be joining them to paddle across the lake. After that they went off to go down a natural water chute. The other therapist could not swim and here she was going down into deep water, a very daring thing to do even though the instructor would be in the pool below. When she was telling me this story I asked, "What did you do?"

Her reply was: "Well, like a good Catholic girl, I said a little prayer, crossed myself and let go." That night, as the therapists were lying in their beds in the hostel, they were listening to the boys chatting in the room next door. They heard the following:

"See them two, they're not bad for two auld dolls!"

Not very flattering for my two thirty-year-old therapists!

Our director of studies always said therapy was not successful if you treated the symptom and not the cause. For example, when assessing a child with speech and language disorder you would request an audiogram if you suspected there was hearing loss. You would always check the tongue and palate to exclude tongue-tie or short soft palate. If you were seeing a five-year-old child and the comprehension, expressive language and articulation tests all came out at a three-year-old level you would request a referral to an educational psychologist for an intelligence test; if the child was functioning at a three-year-old level, therapy would be contraindicated.

Sometimes, especially with stammering or voice disorders, it was important to find out if there were any factors in the person's life which would have a bearing on the problem. When I was treating patients with a stammer, in the initial consultation, I stressed that no attention was to be drawn to the speech. Parents or family members were not to say 'go slowly', 'take a deep breath', 'don't do that' or 'say it over again'. At initial interview I would also try and find out if there were any factors that the parents felt would be affecting the child, such as the family situation, any illness, or worries about school. And unless the stammer was very severe, I would arrange to see the child in a few months' time to see if the situation had improved. But I would advise the parent that if the stammer suddenly got worse to contact me immediately. I remember one child in particular, a little girl named June. She was seen and advised and I reviewed her six months later. The mother had followed the advice and the stammer was practically non-existent. I arranged to see her in six months' time, but again I emphasised to contact me if there was a problem. About a month later the mother did contact me. June had started to stammer again and the mother could think of no reason why. After talking with June, I discovered that she had gone to see the *Wizard of Oz* and was frightened at night after seeing the wicked witch. We talked about this, drew some pictures etc and I advised the mother to have a little night-light for a while. June's speech settled down. I was only contacted once more by the parent a number of months later. The problem this time was that June's best friend had been promoted to the grade 'A' reading group in school and June was upset about this. I discussed this with the school teacher and discovered June would also be moved up in a few weeks' time. However, the teacher expedited this and June was moved up immediately. The stammer ceased. I think that was the last time I saw the child, her speech was normal.

There is a lot of talk about children who are left-handed having problems with a stammer. I know that many years ago children were forced to use their right hand for writing and this was a problem for them. I don't think this would happen now, I hope not!

One day one of my patients, Johnny Brown, told me how his teacher was making him use his right hand and how hard it was for him as he was punished for bad writing. When Johnny left the clinic that day I phoned the headmaster of his school and explained the problem. The headmaster said he would speak to the teacher concerned. A few hours later I received a phone call from the headmaster to say that he had gone to the teacher and explained the situation. The teacher then called Johnny up and told him he could now use his left hand. Johnny started to cry.

He said, "I don't want to use my left hand. I can't write with it." So there they were two teachers looking at a boy crying and saying that he didn't want to use his left hand. The headmaster then phoned me to tell me what had happened. Needless to say I was amazed.

Johnny had definitely told me he couldn't write with his right hand and was now upset and crying when told that he didn't have to. The headmaster and I discussed this and eventually we discovered what you may have already guessed, there were two Johnny Browns in the school, and the headmaster had gone to the wrong one! Problem solved!

Angela was one of the children I remember very well. She was first referred to me when she was about eight years old. She had a stammer and a 'lisp'. She was very attractive, very intelligent and slightly plump with lovely golden curly hair and a delightful nature. Her parents had not sought treatment as her stammer wasn't too bad, but as it was becoming worse they were anxious to have some help. Unfortunately the problem was trying to find a suitable time for her to attend. The only time her father could bring her was twelve o'clock on a Thursday and that was very difficult for me. An assessment clinic had been set up in a nearby school and I was only working part-time. Every Thursday a bus brought a number of children from the assessment clinic. While the bus was meant to arrive at ten o'clock and leave at twelve, often it did not arrive on time and it meant that treatment for Angela couldn't start until quarter past twelve and the father had to leave again for work. I was unable to change the bus immediately and the father eventually failed to bring Angela for treatment. When I phoned to speak to the father I was told that they were making other arrangements.

About a year later one of the health visitors came to see me. She had been doing a school visit that day. One of the teachers had spoken to her about Angela. Apparently her speech was very, very bad. She was unable to get any words out and was now stamping her feet when she got stuck on words. I told the health visitor what had happened and that I would send a further appointment but it was up to the parents. This time I was able to offer a time that suited them and Angela attended for treatment. She had actually been seen by someone else during the previous year, it was not a speech therapist, but I was never able to determine who it was or what their profession was.

One day during our treatment we were discussing Angela's stammer and she told me it was all because of 'the monster'. So she drew 'the monster' for me. She took a piece of paper and she scribbled all over it, every single bit of it and in the middle she drew a little stick figure. She explained that this was her in the middle and that all this black was the monster who had swallowed her. I asked her how this had happened and she told me that one day on holiday they had gone to the park and she had fallen off a swing. She said her knee was very badly cut and the monster had got in that day. At the end of my treatment that morning I spoke to her father. In my notes there was no mention of this accident and in fact the parents were unable to remember when the stammer had started. When I mentioned the accident to the father he said yes, he did remember the time her leg was quite badly cut and that she had to have some stitches.

Angela continued to attend each week and we would do all the usual treatment, relaxation and prolonged speech etc. And each week we would talk about how she was doing at school. However, periodically she would ask me, "Would you like me to draw the monster?" As her speech improved the scribbles on the page became less and less, until one day she drew the picture and in the middle of a clean white page she drew something a bit like a mouse and beside it she wrote: *He's tame now.*

I met Angela many years later; she had been to university and was actually working in a profession that demanded her to communicate with the public. I was delighted to see her speech was normal. She was a lovely girl.

Mrs Martin came to the clinic one day with her daughter Caroline. Caroline had always had a very slight stammer but nothing that bothered anyone but suddenly about aged fourteen the stammer became much worse. Her mother was very concerned and brought her to the clinic. As usual I enquired if anything had happened recently to upset her and to bring on the stammer. Her mother was unable to account for anything. I arranged for Caroline to come for treatment.

She had only been attending for a few weeks when I discovered what the problem was. Caroline had recently started menstruating. Her mother had explained, as many parents may have done in those days, that at this time of the month she was never to get her hair wet or to wash it and never ever to wash her feet because if she did she may end up with mental problems. Caroline knew nothing about the facts of life and naturally was quite frightened by it all. The following Saturday morning in town I bought two little booklets which I brought to the clinic. The following week I told her mother what I was intending to do. I also explained to Mrs Martin that what in fact she had been telling her daughter were 'old wives' tales'. I explained to Caroline that at this time of the month it was most important to wash herself including her hair and feet! I gave the little booklets to Mrs Martin and said if she had any problems that she was to discuss them with me.

About Mrs Martin herself, she was, I think, a hypochondriac. Nearly every week when she came in she would tell me that on their way home she was going to call in to see the doctor. She was very hesitant to explain what was wrong; for example: if it was anything to do with her breasts she would just lower her eyes to the general direction. If there was anything else, her eyes would just go down a little bit further and you knew what she meant! One day she came in and said something was wrong and so her eyes went down to her breasts.

The following week I asked her, "Well Mrs Martin, what did the doctor say?"

She said, "Oh Mrs Shaw I feel terrible. He said, 'Mrs Martin if there is ever anything wrong with you, we will certainly know about it in time'."

Her daughter Caroline was able to be discharged from therapy not very long after that.

When I started work in the hospital I really loved treating patients with voice disorders, for example, hoarseness (dysphonia) which is usually caused by misuse of the voice, (we were told at college that it is typical of a sergeant-major who shouted instructions to the troops); nodules on the vocal cords which are often experienced by singers, or boys whose voices do not 'break'; total loss of voice which is often due to a psychological problem and laryngectomy when the larynx is removed due to disease e.g. cancer.

The one aspect of the work I did not like was that with patients who had a laryngectomy. When the larynx is removed patients would have a tracheostomy. To speak, breath needs to come into your mouth or nose and after a tracheostomy this is not possible. The treatment for this was for the patients to swallow air and then return it i.e. 'burp'. My problem was I was never able to burp! I swallowed gallons of lemonade in an effort to do this, but never really managed to do it properly, so I ended up with something that I thought sounded like a burp but wasn't.

I remember one patient I treated, a lovely man, called Mr Dawson. The prognosis in his case was actually very poor. He had cancer of the larynx and glands of the neck and had been given three months to live. However, the family decided to take him to a private clinic overseas and he had an operation to remove the cancer. When I first saw him the prognosis was still not good. His wife brought him weekly for treatment and he developed speech which was effective but, shall we say, did not sound very good! As it happened I was getting married at the time and leaving the service and Mrs Dawson said that she was very happy with his speech and the service we provided. She did not want onward referral to another therapist. I think one of her reasons may also have been the fact that the prognosis was so poor.

About seven years later I was on holiday in Northern Ireland with my family. We were sitting in the dining room for lunch one day and I heard this voice. Immediately I knew that it was Mr Dawson. Nobody else could talk like that! I went over and spoke to him. He was there with his son and grandson. They were on holiday like myself. His wife had died a few years previously. It was lovely to see him again for it is not often we see patients years later. I think he lived a few years after that.

The other disorder which the College of Speech Therapists includes under voice is what is called resonance. This would include children or adults with too much nasality (hypernasality) or too little nasality (hyponasality). Too much nasality usually occurs as a result of cleft palate, when the air coming from the lungs is not directed into the mouth but is directed into the nose. Hyponasality is usually the result of a child with enlarged adenoids when the air is blocked from coming down the nose and it sounds like you're saying 'plub-jab' instead of 'plum-jam' or 'I have a cold in my dose'.

When I increased my sessions from four to five I was asked if I would go to work in an ESN school i.e. a school for slow-learners. One of the children who was sent up to me for assessment, came in and when I asked his name he said what sounded like: 'Ami Among'.

I could not make this out and one of the other children there told me his name was actually Tommy Armstrong. He was thirteen years old, with totally unintelligible speech. I checked his mouth and sure enough he had a very short soft palate. I sent a note home with him and asked his mother to come see me at the school the following week, which she did. I asked why nothing had been done about Tommy's speech before this and why nothing had been done to treat this problem. She said that she had been worried and that he had been five times to the hospital for a DAWO (Double Antrim Wash Out). In other words, they were treating him as if he had a sinus problem instead of a short soft palate. It is perhaps wrong to criticise the doctors for this, as the hospital he had been referred to did not have a speech therapist and the doctors who had been treating him probably did not understand the nature of the problem. Doctors at that time received no training at all about speech therapy. Tommy was immediately referred to the plastic surgeon. He had his operation and was taken on for treatment. He progressed well.

Then there was Harry. He also had a short soft palate and wasn't treated until he was about five years old. He attended for therapy and improved very well. A few years later he was scheduled for review at the cleft palate clinic at the hospital but he didn't attend. When he didn't attend the second appointment the therapist at the hospital contacted me and asked me if I could see why he wasn't attending. So, I went over to his house and spoke to the father. This was the early 1970s, the height of the 'The Troubles' in Northern Ireland. The father's response was:

"Do you want to get me killed?! Do you think I'm going to go up there where I could be shot at or anything?"

So I asked:

"Well do you mind if I take Harry to the clinic?"

"Not at all love, take him if you want!" he replied.

I told him I would arrange an appointment and let him know when I would come for Harry. As I came away from his house, I thought to myself he obviously doesn't care if I get shot or caught up in a bomb, but he obviously doesn't worry about Harry either.

As it happened I ended up taking three children to the hospital that day. I remember the plastic surgeon asking me if I was covered by insurance. I had never even thought of that. He then said:

"I can just see you in court saying, 'Well your honour, it was like this – I was just going down the road and there happened to be three cleft palate patients standing at the bus stop and I gave them a lift!'"

After this incident I made sure that I was always covered by insurance.

I can't remember what year it was, but I was invited by the College of Speech Therapists to join a working party on statistics. I quite enjoyed these trips to the College as over the years I had been involved with various projects and had got to know many of the therapists. The project this time was to determine what statistics were actually essential to collect. The initial list that was put up on the blackboard consisted of ninety pieces of information. This was obviously far too much and had to be prioritised. So off we started. We agreed that the first pieces of information which were necessary to collect, were whether a patient was new to the service or already attending, i.e. 'N' or 'O' (new or old). Then the next three lines were headed 'M', 'F' and 'O'. So, there I was, looking at this and thinking, what does 'M', 'F', 'O' stand for? Obviously 'Male' and 'Female' but what was the 'O' for? I did not know there was such a thing as 'Other'!

"Excuse me," I asked, "what does the 'O' stand for?"

Everyone laughed and said, "Oh Eleanor! It stands for 'Other' of course!"

Naive to the last, I said, "I didn't know there was such thing as 'Other'!"

Apparently at that time in England (never in Ireland that I knew of) they were having a number of transgender patients with voice problems. Male-to-female voices were too low, and female-to-male voices were too high. People were attending for speech therapy to correct the pitch of the voice.

Fifty years ago, children with severe problems were termed 'Severely Sub-normal'. Children who were 'slow learners' were deemed 'Educationally Sub-normal'. Both attended special schools. In 1974 when I took up post, the provision for all the special schools and training centres, including Muckamore Abbey (at that time a 900 bed hospital), was one session per week. There had been a full time speech therapist appointed for Eastern Special Care and had worked there for some time, however, she had left and not been replaced so the service had been reduced to one session. While the parents, teachers and instructors were crying out for therapy for their centres, it wasn't generally recognised that speech therapy was a priority for this category of patient.

One of the first changes I made on becoming the Area Therapist was to encourage the therapist doing the one session to increase her hours. This she did. In the September of 1974 three new therapists graduated. These girls had all been on bursaries. Each of them undertook some sessions with special needs in the District they were to work. I am glad to say that gradually the service for these vulnerable children and adults was increased.

I cannot remember what year it was, but I was at a meeting and I was introduced to the then Minister of Health. My line manager at that time introduced me to him and if I remember correctly said something like:

"You had better watch her, or she'll bend your ear about the lack of speech therapists!"

I am glad to say that I did 'bend his ear', as that year in the budget we were given funding for twenty speech therapists exclusively for services to special needs in Northern Ireland. Twelve of these posts came to Eastern Board.

I would like to pay tribute here to Mrs Evelyn Greer, the then Director of Mencap in Northern Ireland, who often provided funding for special training for therapists working with special needs children and adults.

Evelyn was always interested in promoting services for the children attending Mencap, and to say that she 'plagued' me to provide speech therapy for the school was putting it mildly. However, having said that, when I was able to provide a service for her I think I in turn probably 'plagued her' for funding for training. When new therapists started work with this category it was often very new to them. Our first major training course took place about 1978. I had been very lucky, two years before that, to employ a speech therapist who was very experienced in working with children and adults with special needs. Unfortunately, about 1978, she was leaving Northern Ireland and I persuaded Mrs Greer to allow me to run a three-day course exclusively for therapists working in this field. It was very successful.

To show the improvement in the service, in 1974 there was 0.1 whole time equivalent speech therapy provision for special needs. When I left the service in 1991 there would have been about twenty full-time therapists working in this field.

In 1975 I had a total of nine therapists for the whole service (7.2 whole time equivalent), when I left I think the figure was one hundred and twenty-five therapists (87.5 whole time equivalent).

The therapist I met in Cardiff who came to work full-time with children with physical disabilities drew my attention to the need for training in feeding these children. As this problem also applied to many children with special needs, I 'persuaded' Mrs Greer to provide funding for a course in feeding. I remember it cost £500 and twenty therapists from across Northern Ireland attended. The therapists then in turn provided training to the staff in the schools and centre where they worked.

We all know about the sign language used by the deaf but thirty-five years ago we introduced Makaton – a sign language for use with those with special needs. Eventually not only the therapists but teachers, physicians, parents and family members all had training in this.

After I became the Area Speech Therapist I became very involved in providing training for speech therapists and also for members of other professions. Very often we would bring parents along to talk about their experiences with their child. One of the people I remember particularly well was Mrs Lamb. Mrs Lamb's first baby, whom she had when she was twenty-two, suffered from Down's syndrome. This is not very usual, generally speaking, children with Down's syndrome are born to older mothers. Mrs Lamb was told that if she had another baby it would probably not have Down's syndrome. However, when the second child was born it also had Down's syndrome. Mrs Lamb told the audience that day the problems of having children with Down's syndrome, but she also emphasised the amount of love, joy and happiness that they had received from these children. She also emphasised that if she became pregnant again and the same thing happened it would not worry her. This is so different to many parents who are in similar positions.

One morning when I was treating a girl who was attending me for treatment of a slight speech disorder, her mother mentioned that the younger child in the family, aged three, was not talking at all. I suggested that she brought Audrey the following week and I would assess her. During the assessment the following week I felt Audrey probably had quite a low IQ. I explained to the mother that since Audrey was a new referral, the clinical medical officer would have to see her and she agreed to this. The following week when the mother brought the older child for treatment, Audrey was seen by the clinical medical officer, who confirmed my suspicions. The clinical medical officer told me later that he had explained the situation to the mother and told her he was referring Audrey to an educational psychologist. The mother agreed to this. The following two weeks the mother did not attend the clinic. Since they had not missed any of their appointments before I felt that something was wrong, so I sent a letter to the mother and asked when would be convenient to attend again. The following week I received a letter from the father saying that they were very annoyed at what had happened to their young daughter and that they had no wish to attend in the future. Not very long after that I found out that the family had actually moved from our area and the children were to attend different schools. Perhaps the parents did not realise that school medical records were in fact transferred to other clinics. The child was later found to have special needs. It is very sad when parents are unable to accept the problem because so many of these children do bring a lot of love with them.

11

Laterality

Everyone knows whether they are right or left-handed and some people know when they are ambidextrous, but very few people know which eye or foot is their dominant one.

Our brains are in two halves, the left side of the brain controls the right side of the body and the right side controls the left. A few people are what is called 'cross lateral'. This is when they use their right hand, for example, but will predominantly use their left eye or foot.

I was always interested in this as I found that a high proportion of children with language disorders were cross lateral and I invariably checked this when I was doing my assessments. The eye is usually checked by rolling up a piece of paper into a tube shape and asking the child to look at something in the room. Invariably they will put it up to the dominant eye. Handedness is checked by asking which hand the child uses to comb their hair, deal out cards, cut something etc. Footedness is checked by asking the child to hop or to kick a ball and I used to think it was funny to write down 'he kicks with his right foot' or 'he kicks with his left foot' because of the religious connotation in Northern Ireland.

When it came to reading I found that children who were cross lateral had problems with reading, they would read words back-to-front much longer than the average child. For example, they would read 'saw' as 'was' and 'on' as 'no'. I felt that this was a problem of scanning that because of their laterality they did not move from the left side of the page to the right side as they should. One of the ways I tried to help them with this was, I would draw pictures on a page and below have a sentence for the picture. For example, if I drew a dog on the left side of the page and a cat on the right I would have the following sentence below with a blank space in between for the child to fill in:

A dog _chases_ a cat.

A cat _chases_ a mouse.

A mouse _runs into_ a hole.

The children would then have to draw lines from each picture.

Another exercise I would give the children was I would draw coloured balloons or balls down the left side of the page and ask them to draw a line to correspond with the same coloured balloon or ball on the other side of the page. I progressed from these simple exercises to more advanced work, but I was always very conscious that I was really not doing what I should be doing as a therapist. In my opinion, what I really needed was an occupational therapist to assess these children and to treat them with me.

1 2

Speech and Language Centre

In 1978 I heard that the clinic in which I had been working was moving to a new health centre. I thought long and hard about this and eventually put in a proposal to the District Medical Officer. What I was proposing was that the clinic would become a Speech and Language Therapy Centre, not only to cope with the current case load, but provide intensive courses of treatment for children with severe speech and language problems.

Speech therapy is a recognised medical service, yet children with severe problems were and still are, sent to special schools for treatment. I simply do not understand that!

My proposal asked for funding for two senior speech therapists (senior one grade at that time) plus an occupational therapist. The children for the intensive course would attend for six weeks of intensive therapy. I also proposed that a teacher would be made available from Belfast Education and Library Board in order for the children to continue their education while they were on the course. The children would attend for approximately five hours a day. The proposal regarding the teacher had already been discussed with the Principal Educational Psychologist and he was willing to provide a remedial teacher. My thanks must go at this point to the Belfast Education Psychology Service for their help and support over the years.

To my surprise and delight my proposal was accepted and the centre was set up in 1980. I was fortunate to find two excellent speech therapists. The Occupational Therapy post was more difficult to fill, as I was told that this type of service had never been provided by an occupational therapist before. However, I was again very fortunate to find a very enthusiastic occupational therapist who advanced this work and was a great asset to the unit.

We had excellent support as I said from the Belfast Psychology Service and from the teaching profession in general. We were eventually receiving referrals from teachers in South-East Education and Library Board as well.

In 1984 there were major changes in the delivery of the Health and Social Services. The six Districts in Eastern Board were abolished and replaced by fourteen units of management. So this, in turn, meant fourteen Unit Managers, fourteen Personnel Departments, etc. etc. Each of these units was to have a speech therapist who would be responsible for the day-to-day management of the service in their unit. As there were only speech therapists in nine of the units at that time I ended up with nine Unit Managers. This involved considerable training for them plus monthly management meetings. This meant that I was unable to take the same amount of interest and be as involved with the centre as I had been previously. The intensive therapy courses were a great achievement and I am only sorry that due to circumstances beyond my control the project was not written up and the results not presented to the College of Speech Therapists. I think if they had realised the results we were getting it might have meant a change in how children with severe speech defects were to be treated in the future. The centre continued to provide intensive therapy until I left the service in 1991.

13

October Speech and Language Month

At the end of the '70s I started receiving letters from Diana Law, the founder and chairman of Action for Dysphasic Adults. Diana had had a very severe stroke herself which left her without speech. Her problems in getting advice and help led her to set up the charity. She was writing to me I think, as well as other therapists across the country to persuade us to have an Interdominational Service for the speech handicapped in October each year. Those of you who know Northern Ireland will realise that for here it was just not as easy as it was on the UK mainland and I did nothing about it initially.

About 1980 a new therapist started employment with Eastern Board. She had worked previously in America or Canada and over there they designated one month each year to highlight services for the speech handicapped. So in 1980 we pursued the idea of running an Interdominational Service. At that time I was a member of the council of the Chest, Heart and Stroke Association and I enlisted their aid.

This was not as easy as it sounds. First of all, I had to find a venue that would be acceptable to all sections of the community. Then I had to arrange for ministers from the different denominations to come and participate. I thought the way to approach a priest was to contact the Bishop of Down and Conor and ask him to suggest someone. Unfortunately I did not know who the Bishop was at that time. The morning I was discussing this, I suddenly realised that a member of our staff, Grainne Donnelly, was actually visiting the clinic.

I went to Grainne and said, "Can you tell me the name of the Bishop of Down and Conor?"

Her reply was, "How would I know?"

I said, "Well, he's your Bishop, you should know."

"How would I know, I'm not a Catholic?" she said.

I joked, "What do you mean you're not a Catholic with a name like 'Grainne Donnelly'."

She said, "I can't help the surname, that came from my father and my mother just liked the name Grainne!"

We eventually got in touch with a priest and ministers from the other denominations who agreed to attend. We contacted a nun who specialised in sign language so that she could interpret for the deaf who we were hoping would also attend. The Inaugural service was held in St. Anne's Cathedral on the first Sunday in October 1981.

On the day of the first service the weather forecast was terrible. People were advised not to go out unless it was essential. I arrived at St Anne's Cathedral feeling that there probably would not be anyone attending beside myself. Despite the terrible weather, we actually had about thirty people in attendance.

Each year after that, for the next ten years, we ran the service the first Sunday in October. Some time before the actual date I would go down to the Cathedral, meet with the Dean and organise the hymns for the day. I would also provide him with the names of those who would read a lesson. We would always have someone with a stammer, someone who was aphasic and someone with a voice problem; usually a laryngectomy and we would sometimes have a choir from one of the special schools.

On the day, staff from the speech therapy department and the Chest, Heart and Stroke Association would arrive early at the Cathedral with biscuits, milk, tea and sugar. We would fill up the large urns to get the hot water and put out the cups and saucers. The congregation were invited to join us after the service for refreshments. The choir boys were always the first down! We left out a special plate of chocolate biscuits for them. Their voices were wonderful. Eventually we were having well in excess of one hundred and fifty attending the service each year.

The success of this meant that I started to think about extending what I did in the month of October. Eventually, after discussions with senior staff and then the rest of the staff, I decided that there would be a theme for each October. It is difficult to remember now the sequence of events but generally we covered one type of disorder each year.

I do remember in great detail some of the programmes we set up. One of these related to children with a physical handicap. The programme that day was really aimed at parents and teachers. What I did initially was contact the services for the blind and got the samples of glasses which demonstrated the different types of eye problems e.g. tunnel vision, partially sighted. We also borrowed wheelchairs and on the morning we sat the parents in turn in the wheelchair while wearing the glasses and wheeled them around an obstacle course at great speed. This was to show them what it was like for their children. The other awful thing the therapists did was they made up bowls of cold porridge which contained curry powder, oil and whatever other nasty things they thought of!

Then we blindfolded the parents and fed them! We were trying to demonstrate what it is like for children who are unable to communicate about the food they do not like. We also did language exercises where we would read nonsense words out to them with the odd word that they did understand. This was to show that even children with limited comprehension can get the gist of what you are saying even if they can understand only a few words. There was one other exercise we did which I used extensively years later when I set up my charity. I did this in small groups during the seminar session.

I would say, "I am going to ask you to do some things now."

I just sat looking at the people, and then said, "Pu dansk."

Everybody would remain sitting there and I could feel them getting uncomfortable.

I would then say, "Saire vou rechs mar," and again, with no response say, "We'll try another one: saire vou flet mar."

Finally I would try the last one, "Sire thob mars."

By this time, everyone was distinctly uneasy.

I would say, "Now we'll try it again."

This time I would say, "Pu dansk," then stand up and indicate an upward movement with my hand. Gradually everyone would stand up.

I said, "Very good," then, "Saire vou rechs mar," and raised my right hand.

Then, "Saire vou flet mar," raised my left hand and "Saire thob mars," where I finally raised both arms.

This demonstrated to people that you didn't have to fully understand what was said, and in fact that gesture played a very big part in our comprehension.

Many years later when I was running the charity, I went to visit one of our patients in the country. Jackie lived alone, his wife had died some time previously. Prior to his stroke he had been a very active man and a very keen gardener. Due to his stroke he was unable to speak, unable to understand what was said to him and unable to read or write, yet he remained very cheerful. When I was there visiting that day, his health visitor came to give him an injection. She asked why I was there and I explained because of his speech problems he would be attending one of our courses.

She looked at me and said, "But Jackie understands every word I say."

I replied, "No, he doesn't understand anything you say."

As she turned round, holding the needle, she said, "Wait and see, c'mon Jackie, roll up your sleeve," and he did. She said, "There, he understood."

I said, "No he didn't. He has not lost his intelligence; he knows that when you come, he will get an injection. Would you like to check this out? I want you to look sad at Jackie, I don't want you to look at the window where you can see his roses, just look at him and say, 'Your roses are really lovely this year, Jackie, plenty of sun.'"

Jackie nodded and frowned and said, "Aye, aye aye."

Now I said, "Will you look happy and say 'terrible what the rain did to your roses this year.'"

He frowned and nodded to her and said, "Aye, aye, aye."

She was really quite shocked.

That course for the physically disabled was very successful and the parents and teachers said how much they had gained from getting to experience what their children had been feeling.

I'm sure if any older therapists read this they will remember that many years ago there was some confusion between teachers and speech therapists over the word 'language'. Both professions felt that language was something that they dealt with. What we as therapists had to convey to teachers was that we were not concerned with the enrichment and structure of language, we were concerned with language that was delayed or deviant.

One year we decided that we would have 'language' as the theme for that October. One of our therapists agreed to do a video demonstrating the work of a speech therapist with language. It covered both adults and children. It lasted one hour and was very good.

What usually happened when we decided to run one of these courses was we would set up a small committee of therapists specialising in that area of work to decide on the programme. We would think about how many people were likely to attend. I would go to a hotel or hospital to arrange the venue, organise a date and work out the cost for the day. The cost would include any materials we would need, lunch and morning coffee. We gave consideration to how many were likely to attend and then divided the total cost by that number in order to give the exact cost of the course. I did not intend at any time to make a profit.

The conference on 'language' was held at the Conway Hotel. I estimated we might have one hundred people in attendance so all the costings were based on that number. In fact, we had two hundred and five delegates including teachers, educational psychologists and education inspectors. It was very, very successful. One of the best conferences we ever had.

Another year, as part of October Speech and Language month, we had a 'Phone In'. A social services department allowed us to use their premises for a whole day. I had approximately six staff there on a rota basis from 9 a.m. to 9 p.m. I went on the radio at 8 a.m. that morning to give details of the 'Phone In' and I also appeared on television later that day to further publicise the event. We were amazed at the response. We had phone calls from every part of the British Isles and the Republic of Ireland. I was surprised to find out how many people listened to Radio Ulster. The phone calls continued to come in for the next two days.

I can remember incidents from some of our other courses, some of which I thought were quite funny. We had two lecturers come over to run a three-day training course for therapists. On the first evening a colleague and I joined the lecturers for a drink after the course. They were both drinking whiskey so we asked if they had ever tried 'Black Bush', a whiskey which is produced in Northern Ireland. They hadn't, so they tried it and thought it was lovely. One of the lecturers then said that what he would really like to try was 'Poteen'. In Northern Ireland somebody always knows somebody who knows somebody who can get you what you want. My colleague did know somebody who knew somebody and the following day she had the 'Poteen'!

That evening we had a course dinner. My colleague Jill and I were coming over to the hotel and she put the 'Poteen' in her handbag. During 'The Troubles' in Northern Ireland there was a security man standing at the door of all hotels. Handbags were always checked when you arrived. As we entered the security man said:

"Open your bag."

Jill opened it and he lifted out the bottle and said:

"What is this?"

Jill replied, "It's a sample."

He dropped the bottle back into her bag like it was a hot potato and told her to go on in. He didn't even look in my bag. Of course this made a very good story for whenever we came to meet up with the lecturers.

The course finished the following day and the lecturers went off home. That night I received a phone call from one of them. As usual, going through the airport, their bags were searched. He remembered the story from the night before, so when the woman asked him what was in the bottle he said:

"It's a sample."

This time, the woman who was searching him just looked at him, laughed and said:

"Get away on with you!"

He enjoyed the poteen.

Over the years, October Speech and Language Month developed considerably. Training schools always insisted that students who applied to do speech therapy visited a speech therapist before their interview. With the degree course at Jordanstown and a further degree course in Dublin, more and more girls were applying to the universities. Unfortunately, it was very difficult to offer all these girls a visit to the clinic. What we decided to do was that each of the six Districts would have one day in the month when local schools would be invited to send anyone interested in doing speech therapy to attend. We had numerous girls coming and very few boys. They would see videos of our work, the kind of tests we used and meet with the therapists.

Finally each year we published leaflets in connection with whatever the particular theme had been.

Eventually the College of Speech and Language Therapists became interested in what we were doing and decided that a month was too long and changed it from October Speech and Language Month to 'Speak Week' which was held in March.

One other story from those days was relating to work that we were doing with adult patients. We had heard of a speech therapist who was doing work with 'icing'. This was used with people following a stroke or head injury who had paralysis on the face. (I understand that this treatment is no longer in use.)

When the therapist arrived to give the talk, the first thing that she said was:

"When I am doing this I use a vibrator," and she produced the thing.

Well! Northern Ireland was a very conservative society, even shall we say, 'straight-laced'. I don't think anyone there that day had ever really seen or heard of vibrators before and we were all feeling very uncomfortable. To elaborate, when the first sex shop opened in Northern Ireland years ago, it didn't last very long because when it opened there were people outside singing hymns and quoting the bible. I don't think anyone would have dared approach the shop.

I heard from the therapist later what happened when she was leaving Northern Ireland. Of course her luggage was searched. The vibrator was lifted out of the case and she was asked what it was. The searcher appeared quite shocked when she found out what it was. The therapist felt she should explain that she only used it for working with patients. However, she didn't think the searcher believed her and she thought she heard the woman say as she was walking away, "Huh, patients my eye."

14

1980s – A Hectic Decade

As more therapists were appointed following the first graduates from Jordanstown and more on secondment were returning to Northern Ireland, I found that my clinical work was being cut down. I felt it was very important that newly qualified therapists should not be left to their own devices. I organised for them to attend once a month for meetings with their colleagues to discuss problem patients and I would always go and see a difficult patient with them. My other commitments included being on the committee TASTM and a number of college committees e.g. one on statistics and eventually one on language. I was involved with the University of Ulster interviews for the course and examining students. Being the most senior therapist in Northern Ireland, purely as a result of 'being responsible' for the largest population, I was always called on as an independent assessor for senior posts. I was on the committee of the Irish District of the Scottish area of the College of Speech Therapists, (eventually to become the Irish District). This involved me attending meetings four times a year with colleagues from the South. These meetings were usually held in Monaghan being a halfway point and I must say during all the time of 'The Troubles', I always dreaded having to go down there, especially if I had to go there on my own. During the winter time that long road from Monaghan to Armagh was quite dark and scary.

In 1984 we were due to a have a further reorganisation of the Health and Social Services. The area paramedical officers in the Eastern Board and I had a series of meetings with the Chief Medical Officer relating to how the Eastern Board was to be divided up. Our feelings were that the six Districts should remain. We felt that people were just getting used to the changes made in 1973. The original change, ten years earlier, was a massive one and it was very difficult at the beginning for people to become used to this change. However, when the plans eventually came out it showed the Eastern Board, instead of being six Districts, would become fourteen Units of management. This meant that instead of having, for example, seven personnel departments, one for Area Board and one for each of the Districts, there would now be fifteen, one for Area Board and one for each of the new Units. This also applied to the finance departments, supplies etc. It was also recommended that in each Unit there would be senior paramedical and speech therapy officers in charge of day-to-day management. I did not have enough staff for all fourteen Units and ended up with nine managers.

The disruption to services at this time was considerable. Each one of the departments had to be increased. In some cases new premises had to be found. All staff had to get used to what had been a considerable upheaval in administration. New stationery had to be printed for all fourteen Units and the cost of this alone was considerable.

I think it was in 1984 I received a call from Mrs Greer at MENCAP to tell me that the 'Seventh International

Conference for People with Mental Handicap' was to be held in Kenya that year. She said that there was no speech therapist on the list of people to attend and she wondered if I could get permission to go.

A request like this had to go firstly through my line manager but then it had to go through the Department of Health and Social Services. I was eventually given permission on condition that on my return a full report on the conference would be presented to the Department and relevant staff. Of course I agreed.

The conference itself was very, very interesting. I had an opportunity to meet with people with special needs and with their relatives. Speech therapists at that time were very few and far between and I spent a considerable amount of time giving advice.

One day we visited a school for children aged, I think, four to sixteen. It was amazing to see this school and compare it to what we had in Northern Ireland. The children had few books and very few toys. The playground consisted of some car tyres and some wood, resulting in a couple of swings, and very little to play with. The teachers in the school were desperate for knowledge on how to help children with speech defects. One parent who was visiting the school that day came over and asked me if he could bring his son over to Northern Ireland to get treatment. What I arranged to do was to send him information on how to help his son, Albert. I also promised to send information to the teachers.

When I returned home the report was submitted to the Department. I arranged a meeting for the staff who were working with children and adults with special needs and gave them copies of lectures that had been given. The chief speech therapist working in this field sent information leaflets to both the school and to Albert's father.

Two other wonderful events happened in the 1980s. In 1986 my daughter Valerie got married to Malcolm. It was a very happy occasion. Two years later, my first grandchild, Claire was born. I felt at the time that the nine months waiting for the birth were probably the longest nine months I had spent in my life. I couldn't wait for the birth of my grandchild. I went up to see the baby a few hours after she was born and came home to tell my mother who was equally as excited about it. I told her the baby was just beautiful. I had seen all the other babies in the nursery and they were all red but Claire wasn't. She was a lovely colour. Of course when I saw the photographs afterwards I realised Claire was as red as all the other babies, I just didn't see it.

Over the next few years my daughter produced another four children: Stephen, Gareth, Patrick and Bethany. They were all lovely!

Sometime in the late 1980s I was asked to go to a meeting with senior health visitors. At that time health visitors and clinical medical officers would go round schools medically examining children in their first year and before they left at age eleven. However, if there were any problems they would be reviewed and if necessary referred to an appropriate doctor or hospital therapist.

The health visitors wanted to know if I could devise some kind of speech and language test that would be easy for them to administer. At that time they had no idea whether to refer a child or not. We discussed this at length and I said that I would do my best to come up with something suitable.

Shortly after that, I invited two of my senior staff who specialised in this area of work to join me in drawing up a test. It took some time but we eventually came up with a test that we felt would be easy to administer. It consisted of a booklet showing pictures which covered nearly all the sounds that children should be using and then some pictures which demonstrated a child's language ability. In order to do this we actually needed some small toys and most of these were impossible to find. It was easy to buy a horse, dog, bear, spoon and a man. However, some toys were more difficult, for example, a small bed, a small house and a chair. We eventually solved the problem by going to the young offenders' centre. It was agreed that they would make the toys for us, at a cost of course and eventually the first Cherryville Speech and Language Test was available. Some time later we did a revision of the test which I understand is still being used by health visitors throughout Northern Ireland.

I worked very closely with MENCAP in Northern Ireland and one day I was surprised to receive an invitation to attend the fortieth anniversary of the founding of MENCAP. The celebration was to be held in St James' Palace and was to be hosted by Queen Elizabeth, the Queen Mother.

On the evening in question there was a heat wave in London. The group from Northern Ireland arrived at St James' Palace and were taken to a large room upstairs. There was a long table filled with the most delicious canapés. We were offered drinks and I had a glass of wine. There were beautiful Georgian windows in the room and the sun was pouring in. It gradually got hotter and hotter. We had another glass of wine. Time went on. The next time I decided to have an orange juice, then another orange juice. I happened to mention I was feeling a little bit 'tiddly'. Well it turned out we were drinking Bucks Fizz. By the time the Queen Mother reached our room, we were all exhausted and perspiring profusely. When the Queen Mother came in she looked so cool and collected despite the fact our party was in the third room that she had attended.

When Mrs Greer introduced me she said, "This is Eleanor Gildea, she is a speech therapist from Northern Ireland."

Her Majesty said, "A speech therapist. I am sure you know how grateful I am to the speech therapy service. You will know that my late husband had a stammer and it was thanks to a speech therapist that he was able to recover." Another wonderful evening.

There always seemed to be a shortage of money in the Health Service. The usual reply I received when I wanted a new post was, "Sorry there is no money." However, I must be fair and say that whenever I made out a case for a new therapist the money was always found.

There was one sure way of obtaining funding and that was when a new facility was being planned; e.g. a new health centre, geriatric unit, training centre for adults with special needs or a new hospital. I would submit a proposal detailing the reasons why a speech therapist was required, the grade of post and any additional costs for example equipment or tests. I would give details of client groups to be treated and last but not least the accommodation required.

The Tower Block at the City Hospital was planned long before I became the area speech therapist. However, I put in a retrospective application for two staff. This was eventually agreed. An additional therapist for the Cochlear Implant Department was also agreed.

<u>Additional Services</u>

In my early years in the community I was not anxious to extend services into specialised fields such as for children with special needs or those who were deaf or partially hearing. Working only on a part-time basis meant that I was already seriously understaffed. However, staffing levels did increase, especially after students were graduating from Jordanstown and I began an overview of the service to establish the deficiencies.

The biggest problem as I saw it was the hospital service. In 1974 I was able to secure a therapist for the City Hospital, the first one ever. The following year I employed one at the Ulster Hospital. The service continued to expand until all the major hospitals were covered. I continued to increase the services for those with special needs and with a physical disability.

There were two other services that were a problem: firstly, children with severe speech and language problems, and secondly, children who were deaf or partially hearing. For the first problem I was eventually able to provide a service in a small specialised unit in a local school. The second problem was more difficult to resolve. When I first broached this subject in schools with classes for the hearing impaired the staff were not interested. They felt as they were teachers of the deaf that they did not need speech therapists.

One day it was suggested that I should visit the school for the deaf in West Belfast. I met the Sister in charge. I explained that I wanted to provide a speech therapy service for the school. Well, talk about a welcome! I really thought she was going to get up and hug me. She said, "This is wonderful, a speech therapist, I can't believe it. Oh my goodness, at long last, I have been wanting one for many years." The she suddenly stopped – leaned over and said, "Oh dear will I be able to afford it?" I explained that this post would be funded by the health service so there would be no cost. When I told her that there would be no cost to her she became most ecstatic. "I don't believe it, I really don't, it's just wonderful news."

I came out of the school feeling very good. It was a lovely welcome.

A few years later I was able to arrange for a member of staff to undertake an advanced course on working with the deaf community. Gradually this service extended throughout the Board.

15

A Slight Diversion

The therapists in Eastern Board very often had fun at the expense of our colleagues from across the water. This was mainly due to them being unable to understand some of our 'local' expressions.

Those of you who read the *Belfast Telegraph* years ago would remember John Pepper's column. He would write about Northern Ireland expressions like, 'my mother is in bed under the doctor' or 'I had to go to the doctor with my leg.' These are just a few examples of where our overseas students had problems.

A therapist interviewing a mother and child asked:

"What's the problem Mrs Brown?"

The mother said, "Well I've brought Johnny here, he's got a stoppage."

The therapist sat there thinking, *a stoppage? This child must be unable to go to the toilet, why is the mother bringing him here?*

She was just about to say I think Mrs. Brown you should be seeing an urologist when the mother said, "Sometimes he can't get his words out at all."

At that point the therapist realised she was saying that he had a stammer.

One of my therapists had just had a baby and I suggested to my colleague, who came from England, that we should go at lunchtime to see her and the new baby.

As we went into the hospital I said, "This is terrible; I feel awful coming here with both arms the same length."

She stopped dead and looked at me and said, "Eleanor, your arms are always the same length."

I explained that what I meant was I wasn't bringing a present for the baby.

This same English therapist asked me one day, "Eleanor what does it mean when someone says they are 'not feeling at themselves'?"

She went onto to explain that a patient's mother had said it to her that morning.

I told her that it meant that she was not feeling as well as she normally did. A few weeks later she came in and said:

"You remember you told me that if someone said they weren't at themselves it meant they weren't feeling well? This morning I had a mother in. I asked her about her son and she said, 'he's a great wee boy, the only problem is he's always at himself'."

The same therapist was visiting a home one day. The woman she was interviewing said that her husband was, 'on the brew'.

Sarah was just about to suggest that the woman tried Alcoholics Anonymous when the woman went on to say, "He's a very good man you know and this is the first time he's been out of work."

Sarah realised that the man was probably not an alcoholic and came in to find out what 'on the brew' meant.

One of my speech therapists came in laughing one day to tell me the following incident. She had just been promoted to a chief speech therapist and had phoned down to College Street to ask if she could have a new badge. The badge arrived and without looking at it, she pinned it on. Later that day someone came in and started to laugh and pointed at her badge and said:

"Have you read what is on there?"

Mrs E. Bloggs

Chief Speech The

Rapist

Speech therapists years ago had very few test materials. One of the ones we used in clinics was called the 'Renfrew Action Picture Test' and had been devised by Catherine Renfrew, one of the founding members of the College of Speech Therapists. The test consisted of a number of pictures and as stated, it was to test a child's language ability. For example, the first picture, an easy one, showed a girl skipping and you would ask, "What is the girl doing?" the child was meant to say 'skipping'. A later picture showed a cat that had just caught two mice. The question asked was, "What has the cat just done?" and the answer was to be 'caught the mice'. This was to test if the child could use the irregular past tense and irregular plural. One day I was administering the test and said to the boy:

"What has the cat just done?"

He looked at me, back to the picture, and then back to me.

He leaned closer and whispered, "She has done a loadie."

I gave him one point for getting an irregular past tense!

16

Communication Aids Centre

One morning at the beginning of the 1980s I read an article which stated that the Department of Trade and Industry was intending to provide funding to set up six Communication Aids Centres across the country. I immediately decided that it would be a wonderful addition to our services here in Northern Ireland. I phoned my line manager and asked for her opinion. She felt that we were unlikely to receive the funding in Northern Ireland but suggested that I wrote to her giving all the details and she would pass it on to the Department of Health at Dundonald House.

I wrote out the letter giving her the details I had obtained in the article and my reasons why such a centre would be very beneficial here. This letter was forwarded to the Department of Health and a few days later I was surprised to receive a call informing me that one of the doctors at the Department was very interested in my suggestion and was going over to London to investigate the matter further. A few weeks later I was told that Bob Fawcus, a speech therapist from London, who had been appointed to take charge of the project, would be coming to Northern Ireland to see me to discuss it further.

My immediate problem was if we were granted this funding where would we site the centre. There were a few possible places, one being the Joss Cardwell rehabilitation centre in East Belfast. The problem here was whether this would be easily accessible to people from the West of the Province and also would there be any available accommodation. The Royal Victoria Hospital would have been an obvious choice, being near to the motorways, but again there would have been difficulty with accommodation and parking was a big problem there. My third choice was Musgrave Park Hospital. This had the advantage of being near the motorway and there was very good parking.

When Bob arrived in Northern Ireland I discussed all these venues with him and went to see the site at Musgrave Park. The Unit Administrator had already agreed to provide accommodation if the centre could be sited there. Bob and I had a very useful meeting when we discussed all the issues relating to the setting up, equipment, staffing etc.

I was delighted when I eventually received word that funding would be provided to Northern Ireland. It was a very valuable addition to the service for the province.

Shortly after that, at Bob's suggestion, I went to visit a Communication Aids Centre in London that had been in operation for some time. I was fascinated at the range of equipment they had. I also heard from the speech therapist about how some of these aids had changed people's lives. To give you one example, she told me how one of her clients, a man who had been running a very successful farm breeding pedigree cows, had unfortunately taken a severe illness which left him totally paralysed except for the use of one finger. Using a communication aid, he was able to print out instructions for his wife and for the manager. Gradually his wife was able to learn the business. I heard later that she was able to take over from him when he died some years later.

We decided we would have an official opening for the new centre and invite a 'celebrity' to open it. In that way we hoped we would invite media coverage to publicise the fact that the centre was now in operation. At that time the *Krypton Factor* was appearing on TV and had a high viewer rating. A friend of mine knew Gordon Burns, the presenter, very well and asked him if he would perform the opening ceremony, to which he agreed.

To deviate a little, I want to tell you about the day of the opening. I always wore high heels except when driving the car as it ruined the heels. So when I was driving I drove in my stocking feet. One very wet day, I was driving home and the car in front of me stopped at a pedestrian crossing. I stopped behind it. As I looked in my side view mirror, I saw a car coming down behind me. I remember thinking that he was travelling very fast. I then turned back to check what was happening in front of me. It started to move, I let off my handbrake and the next thing the car behind hit me and I hit the car in front. I immediately bent down to look for my shoes and in my panic couldn't find them. The next thing, the door opened and a voice said, "Are you alright?"

This was an assistant from the shop nearby, who was alarmed when I vanished. He thought I had been hurt. I still couldn't find the shoes so I got out of the car in my bare feet. After that I always wore a pair of old shoes with flat heels when driving, just in case!

Now back to my story of the opening of the centre. I drove down to the hotel in the centre of Belfast, pulled up outside the entrance, lifted my handbag and went in to meet Gordon. When we came out of the hotel I discovered that I had locked the door with the keys inside. So there I was in a pair of scruffy shoes going to this event in Musgrave Park. There was nothing I could do, I had to arrange for someone to open the door, so until then the car sat outside the hotel and we had to get a taxi. When I was talking to the photographers I asked them to make sure not to take any photos of my feet! To crown it all, the plaque which was put on the wall that day had the wrong date on it and could not be seen in the photographs either. We did get extensive media coverage in newspapers and TV. One of the newspaper headlines read, *If you can blink you can talk*. Many children and adults with physical disabilities benefited from the equipment we provided.

17

Committee Work

From 1974 when I became the area speech therapist I was very involved in the Chest, Heart and Stroke Association. This came about because the Association was very keen to start a volunteer stroke scheme similar to the one that they had in England. They also had acquired a number of 'speech tapes' which they wanted to hand to people with aphasia. I was concerned about this as I felt that tapes that were unsuitable could be given to some of these patients. I suggested that the tapes would be given out after the patients were seen by a speech therapist and not directly by a volunteer. After some discussions and negotiations we eventually worked out a scheme that suited us both.

Eventually the Chest, Heart and Stroke Association did set up some groups which covered all stroke patients and not only those with aphasia and some of my staff and I provided training to volunteers. I continued my involvement with the Chest, Heart and Stroke Association until I set up my own charity in 1991.

The other charity that I became involved with was Rubella. Mrs. Greer, the Director of MENCAP, asked for my involvement because children born to a mother who had German measles during her pregnancy had severe disabilities which could involve hearing, sight and speech. I feel that this charity did excellent work encouraging the vaccination of school girls against Rubella.

After a number of years this association joined up with Sense UK. A few years later two residential units for children who were deaf and blind were set up in County Antrim to provide residential care. Princess Anne came to open these centres. I was very impressed with Princess Anne. She had obviously 'done her homework'. She really understood the problems faced by not only the children who were deaf and blind but the problems their parents faced as well. The whole committee felt that she had obviously spent a considerable amount of time learning about the work of Sense UK before she came to open the centre.

I continued my involvement with Sense UK for many years.

I received a phone call one day from the Director of Barnardos to tell me that they were setting up a centre at Carrickfoyle, a house on the Belmont Road. This centre was to deal with very young children with special needs and their parents. I was asked if I would consider being on the committee and I agreed.

Carrickfoyle went on to provide an excellent service for these children and their parents.

One day at the committee meeting we were told that there was to be a party to celebrate Carrickfoyle's fourth birthday. I thought it was a very odd birthday to celebrate but agreed to attend. We were asked to be there by 2 p.m.

On the morning of the party I was at my clinic and I

received a telephone call to say that I should really try and come a bit earlier as there might be a lack of space in the car park. As I was leaving the clinic that morning I had difficulty getting out onto the main road. One of the neighbours (Billy) was standing at his door.

I said, "There's a lot of traffic today, Billy."

And he replied, "Yes, I hear Princess Di is in the province."

I sat there in the car and thought, *oh my goodness, this must be our party*. I drove home as fast as I could, rushed in, touched up my make-up, put on my best dress, tonged my hair and headed off. The Belmont Road was packed. I must say I felt a bit like royalty myself as the police waved me through to the car park.

Princess Diana was absolutely lovely, not only in looks but in her manner. She was wonderful with both the parents and the young children. As the committee, we were able to talk to her, she was charming. The food was laid out in the garden and in the centre was a birthday cake with four candles. A little girl was there to blow them out and unfortunately couldn't reach. Princess Diana bent down, picked her up and held her so she could blow them out. It was a lovely day.

18

Area Therapists

There were Area Speech Therapists appointed to each one of the four areas in Northern Ireland. From the beginning the four of us would meet every few months in a different venue. There were always issues coming up of interest to us all and it was important to discuss these various issues to obtain a consensus. For example, if new legislation or grading was to be introduced.

One of the later issues we dealt with was whether there should be some form of staff appraisal. This was a very thorny issue. We spent many, many months, over numerous meetings, discussing how this should be set out. Eventually the initial draft appraisal form was taken back and shown to senior staff in each of the areas. Amendments were made and brought back to the drawing board. Eventually an appraisal form was agreed. It was then important that each one of the Area Therapists trained their senior staff who would be administering the appraisal to their junior staff. I well remember the day when I went to have my own appraisal done by the assistant Chief Administrative Medical Officer (CAMO) who was my line manager. He was very interested in why we had actually put some of the questions down. I enjoyed that appraisal very much, I think.

One other issue I remember which took up a considerable amount of our time was the organisation of an advanced training course for speech therapists interested in working with children and adults with special needs. Sometime earlier the College of Speech and Language Therapists had decided to offer funding for therapists to take up specialised training in various aspects of our service. In Eastern Board I had a very, very experienced therapist. She contacted other experienced therapists in Northern Ireland in this area of work to enquire if they would be interested in running such a course. They agreed. The Area Therapists were then approached for our approval. Following this a letter was sent to the College and it was agreed that we would run this course. It was eventually held in Londonderry and it was very successful.

Finally, I represented Northern Ireland on a number of committees for example TASTM and working parties at the College in London on child language and statistics. I always reported back at our meetings.

19

Holiday Schemes – A Great Idea

One day at a meeting of staff working in schools I happened to mention that there should be something for children to do during the summer holidays because very often they had reached a stage in their speech at the end of June and would not see a therapist again until September. So the idea emerged of maybe taking some children away on holiday, providing a few hours of therapy each morning and then fun for the rest of the day. The problems that we faced were as follows:

Where would we find a suitable venue?
Would staff be willing to go and how many would we need?
Would we need insurance for the staff?
What about transport, would we get insurance for that?
What arrangements would we make about food etc?
Most importantly who would pay for all of this?

After a great deal of searching I eventually found that one of the large schools had access to a cottage right on the beach in the Ards Peninsula. They were willing to let us have it for one week during the summer. The other problems were easily solved; the staff at the school were willing to go and we had students who also volunteered to help. The issue of transport was a problem but we ultimately solved that as well. Now we came to the money. We decided that we would have a jumble sale and I had permission to have this on a Saturday in my clinic.

We decided to charge £1 admission which gave people tea or coffee, a scone and a tray bake. Where to get the scones and tray bakes? What I did was, I contacted a local bakery which I used. I asked Jim if I got him some flour, would he give me some scones and some tray bakes. He agreed. I then contacted a flour manufacturer in Belfast and he agreed to give me two sacks of flour and to deliver them to the bakery (back to bartering again).

The week prior to the jumble sale, the staff brought used toys, books and bric-a-brac and each room was designated respectively. On the morning of the sale I was at the bakery very early collecting two big trays of cakes and scones.

We had a successful morning raising in excess of £600. This was signed off as correct by our therapists. The money was lodged in a speech therapy account at Eastern Board.

The summer scheme for the children was very, very successful. Some of these children had never been to a beach before and they were fascinated looking for crabs and making sandcastles. Every morning was spent doing speech therapy and each afternoon they were taken out, being July, flags were everywhere. The children, from both sides of the community, wanted flags to stick in their sandcastles. I don't know how some parents would have reacted to this but the children loved it.

This scheme was so successful, from the point of view of improvement of the children, so we decided to widen it. We continued to take a similar group of young children away but the following year we took a group of thirty children with physical disabilities and the following year this was extended again and we took a group of older children to an adventure venue in County Antrim.

I continued the jumble sales. One year we ran an 'Arts and Crafts' fair. We borrowed the Joss Cardwell centre for a Friday night and Saturday morning. Sandwiches and soup were provided for lunch on the Saturday. We made a lot of money, at that particular fair, over £2,000 was raised.

20

Quality Assurance

In all the years I worked I never had a complaint about a therapist or the service we were offering. However, like all other professions I was becoming very aware of the public's interest in litigation and compensation.

At that time a therapist, who worked in schools as I had done, would go into the school and receive lists of children's names that the staff considered needed therapy. The therapist then would bring the children in, assess them and treat them if necessary. Very occasionally a parent would ring up and say that they were interested in this work but that did not happen very often. The children who attended these schools were generally brought there by bus and it could be quite a distance away from their home. Legally the bus driver was not allowed to bring parents and so they would have to find their own way to the school.

I had been thinking about this for some time and decided that legally we should have some kind of policy relating to what happened to children attending schools. Obviously this was very different to children attending in clinics who were nearly

146

always brought by a parent. I brought some of my senior staff who worked in schools to a meeting and told them that I felt we should have policy statements. These became the basis for our quality assurance document. I didn't realise at the time the way this would turn out.

The group I set up considered what we should do regarding referrals for children and regarding the treatment. Without going into this in great detail, our main issues were that parents should be informed and consent received from them before any treatment could be given in the school. In other words, if a parent did not reply to our letter the child would not receive treatment. Further points covered included how teachers were to be informed, the amount of treatment the child would receive and discharge procedures. Having done that for one type of school I extended it to what happened in clinics.

All this was going on over a number of months. It was about six or eight months later that two of my staff attended a meeting at the College of Speech and Language Therapists. They happened to mention what I was doing in Northern Ireland. To their surprise they found that a therapist, Tessa Smith, had just been commissioned by the College to do the same thing but covering all types of disorder.

Tessa got in touch with me and asked if she could come over to Northern Ireland and have a seminar based on what we had been doing already. Of course I agreed and organized a two-day seminar and invited therapists from across Northern Ireland to attend. It was a very successful seminar. The work done those two days formed the basis of the Quality Assurance and Audit Document which I presented to Eastern Board before I left the service in 1991.

I was very honoured in 1987 to receive a letter from the College of Speech Therapists in London informing me that I had been awarded the Honours of the College for my services to it. I cannot express how I felt when I received this letter. I had never in my wildest dreams ever imagined that I would be honoured in this way. I was almost crying when I went in to tell my mother the news. I went to the AGM in Exeter that year to receive the award. I was the first speech therapist in Ireland to be honoured in this way.

21

An Awful Year

In 1989 we were informed that there was to be a regrading for the staff. We all waited with bated breath to see what arrangements were being made. When the regrading came it was very difficult to interpret how it was to be done. Initially it was basically an assimilation i.e. your current grade would be assimilated onto the relevant point on the new scale. The main problem with the new grading was that there was going to be such a huge difference in salary between two of the grades. Basically, the first grade was a senior two, then a senior one and the next point on the scale was a chief three. The difference in salary between the latter two points was something like £3,000. However, the senior one grade you were allowed to have additional points, i.e. there was a senior 1+ or a senior 1++ which allowed extra salary. The new salary scale was not meant to be implemented for some time and of course the Area Therapists had many discussions about it, as did the staff. I am not sure but I think that staff in the personnel departments in the four Area Boards had agreed that the Eastern Board should try and come up with something first and then if acceptable they would follow suit. This put a tremendous responsibility on me.

I had many long discussions with staff and it was impossible to find a consensus. Eventually I decided that one senior member of staff and I would work out something and present it to the others. Needless to say the two of us spent many, many hours trying to work out what we thought was fair.

Eventually we formulated a plan which we felt provided additional salary for people who had more experience. With one hundred and twenty-five staff it would have been impossible to put a large number onto the chief three scales as it would not have been accepted.

When our ideas were finalized I called a meeting of the staff and presented it. To my surprise the first comment came from the union representative who said that our ideas were much better than what she had been expecting. However, and unfortunately, a few members of staff disagreed. They felt that I had not recognized their worth. What I tried to explain over and over again was that I was not regrading the staff, that was not what I had been asked to do, I was asked to grade the posts. Basically that meant that if a therapist left today, her post would be graded as it was when she had been appointed. For example I remember one therapist who was very annoyed with me. She had been appointed two and a half years previously when just newly qualified. She had certainly become more experienced and was a good therapist. She was angry that her post was still going to be a senior two (the basic grade). She simply could not understand that if she left it would stay at the basic grade post. One of the issues that seemed to upset the therapists was that during the assimilation I had been appointed to be the top grade. I think some of the therapists thought that I had negotiated a good deal for myself but not for them. Eastern Board was the second biggest board in the British Isles and that was why I was assimilated to the top post. It was nothing to do with me negotiating a good deal for myself. It was population banding.

This was a terrible, terrible time for me. I found it very distressing that for the first time ever I was having bad relations with my staff.

22

Another Awful Year

January 1990 arrived and with it the new Trusts. Looking back at my diary for that time all I could see were meetings, meetings and more meetings! The problem was that I felt very, very tired. I thought it was due to the extreme stress that I had been experiencing the previous year. I am normally someone with a great deal of energy and I was able to cope with my full-time job, my mother who spent most of her time with me and who was never really very well, my husband who was also unwell and my children, but I suddenly felt exhausted. This went on and on and I felt worse every day. I was really relieved when Easter came and I was able to have a few days off work.

On the Saturday night, I was sitting watching television and rubbing my chin when I suddenly realised that I had very swollen glands. Having heard about glandular fever I wondered if I could possibly have that. I phoned my daughter for her advice. She said that it probably wasn't but to go on Wednesday when the surgery reopened to see my GP. I did, she examined me and said I had swollen glands in my neck, stomach and groin. She took a blood test and told me to phone back on Friday afternoon for the result. On Friday morning at about

8.45 a.m. I received a phone call from the doctor saying that there was a problem with my blood, if my memory serves me correctly she said something about mono-nuclear cells. She had made an appointment for me on the following Tuesday morning at the Haematology department in the Royal Victoria Hospital. I phoned my daughter to tell her and ask her what this meant, she pretended not to know and asked me what I thought it meant.

I said, "I don't know, what do you think it means?"

I of course was thinking that it sounded like I had leukaemia and she knew very well that that was likely to be the diagnosis.

Tuesday morning came and Valerie and I set off for the hospital. We went into see the consultant who said, "Well Mrs. Gildea, do you know why you're here?"

"Yes," I said. "There is something wrong with my blood?"

She said, "Yes, we think you have leukaemia."

Well. What do you say to that? She arranged for me to have a bone marrow procedure and other tests.

A few weeks later I went up to the hospital to have these tests done. I remember very well the bone marrow test which two nurses administered. As I lay on my side one of the nurses came over and said:

"Mrs Gildea, you can scream if you want to, but please don't move!"

I must say, I didn't feel reassured for what was about to happen. Following that I had another test. I don't know what it was called but it involved me drinking a very large quantity of water and then having some kind of scan.

My friend who had taken me to the hospital that day brought me home about 3 p.m. I was feeling totally exhausted.

All I wanted was a cup of tea and to sit down for a while. I came in and my mother told that there had been an urgent call from the new Trust headquarters. I had apparently been meant to attend a meeting. Neither my secretary nor I knew anything about this meeting. I phoned to enquire and was told the Chief Executive and another speech therapist were waiting for me to appear. I of course got into my car, drove up to this meeting which was to discuss my future post.

I remember when I arrived the secretary saying, "Mrs Gildea, you look absolutely awful, are you sure you are alright?"

The meeting that day was to decide whether I would take on the management of South and East Belfast which were now amalgamated. It is very hard to remember all the discussions that day. Basically the speech therapist who was the manager in South Belfast was leaving and the question was, "Would I take on the management of both Trusts?" The newly amalgamated South and East Belfast Trust. I felt it would not be a problem as I had managed the whole area for sixteen years.

I gradually began to feel a little bit better and at the beginning of June I was told that I did not have leukaemia. It was probably a very bad virus. It was a great relief to my family and me.

In the middle of June I had a meeting in London. I returned home that evening and my mother said she had a bit of bad news. My husband Jack had been taken into hospital that day. Initially he had refused to go to the hospital until I had arrived home but had taken so ill that my daughter arranged for an ambulance to take him there.

I went immediately to the Royal Victoria to find Jack attached to a drip. I was told that he was just dehydrated. He was now feeling better and would return home the next day. I went home feeling reassured.

The following morning my secretary said there was a phone call from the hospital. It was the consultant who said that Jack had been found to have a leaking aortic aneurism and was going to have an operation that morning. I said I would come over right away but was told that in view of the situation he had already been sent to the operating theatre. Four hours later I received word that Jack had been transferred to the intensive care unit in the City Hospital. The operation was over but he had 'died' three times during it.

It was a terrible time. Jack was in intensive care completely unconscious for the next two weeks and was then kept in for a further week. It is really very disturbing to go and see someone in intensive care. There seemed to be wires everywhere!

I was going to the hospital two-three times every day. I remember one Saturday coming home at lunchtime and I decided to sit down and have a rest before going back in the afternoon. I sat down on the chair and closed my eyes and suddenly heard what I thought was a bluebottle. It buzzed around me but I couldn't see it. I eventually got up and went and got some fly killer. I sat down on the chair. There was more buzzing, but again no fly. Eventually it dawned on me that it wasn't a fly, it was tinnitus. I decided that I would just rest that afternoon. I was sure that it was just due to tension and nothing else.

After three weeks my husband came home. I brought a bed downstairs for him to make his care easier for me to manage. Six weeks later he decided he wanted to go on holiday. He actually wanted to go to Cyprus, but there was no way he would have been allowed. We went to Scotland instead. Four days into the holiday, he was not feeling well and we had to come home. Four days later at the end of August he died. It really was a very sad, distressing time.

Work wise this was also a terrible time. The area posts were being abolished so technically I was going to be without a job. There were numerous meetings to decide what was going to happen and where people were going to be slotted in. The Trust I was working in wanted me to stay on as manager of South and East Belfast. I had an offer from another Trust to be manager of the Professions Allied to Medicine and my line manager was very keen that I should apply for the post of Director of Community Health in one of the Trusts. I was considering all these options during the time Jack was ill. One day I had a review appointment with the Haematologist. While I was thinking of applying for the new post I was reading a book, 'SURVIVING IN GENERAL MANAGEMENT'.

She asked me why I was reading it and I told her. She asked me if I needed the job.

I asked, "What do you mean by that?"

She said, "Will you get a much higher salary?"

I replied, "I don't know, I didn't ask!"

She said, "My advice to you is to not go for this post unless you really need it. You certainly do not need any more stress in your life at this time."

I came home, I thought about it and I decided that she was probably right. I pulled out of the interview for the Director of Community Health post and I decided to take the management post in South and East Belfast.

For the next month, September, everything went on smoothly. Then a problem arose which unfortunately added greatly to my stress level. I was asked by someone senior to me in management to do something that I considered unprofessional. I said to her, "I am sorry I cannot do that as I consider that to be unprofessional."

I was told, "You will do it." I again explained the reasons why I could not do it and was told again, "Just do it."

I replied, "All right I will do it if you give me this directive in writing." This request was refused.

Understandably relations became tense and this also added to my stress levels. Remember this was just in the month after my husband's death and a few months after I had been informed that I was not suffering from leukaemia.

Eventually I was given a new job description which was totally against what had been agreed. After much thought, I decided to apply for redundancy. This was refused. I was told I was needed!

One morning I received a phone call to tell me to attend a meeting that afternoon to discuss my job description and the redundancy issue.

I took the problem to a senior medical officer, my former line manager. He looked at the job description I had been given and then he told me that under no circumstances was I to go to such a meeting without a representative from the College being with me. He then wrote a letter to the effect that: *'I have today advised Mrs Gildea that she is not to attend any meeting to discuss her job description or redundancy without a representative from her College being present.'*

I had to deliver this letter to the personnel department. It was not a pleasant experience!

The next appointment offered was for a meeting on the 24th December at 3 p.m. Tessa Smith, the representative chosen by the College, agreed to attend at that time but I already had approval for annual leave. The meeting was then rescheduled for the 4th January. Tessa and a very experienced personnel officer from London accompanied me.

It was a very stressful meeting as far as I was concerned. However, at the end of the few hours that it took I was told that a decision would be made shortly. A few weeks later I was told that I would be allowed to take my redundancy package.

Shortly after that I had a severe chest infection. I visited the doctor to get antibiotics and during my appointment with him he said he thought I was suffering from stress and wanted me to take a month's sick leave. I refused to do this but agreed reluctantly to take a week. The doctor insisted on seeing me a week later and at that time he did insist that I took another three weeks' leave. This was the first time in all the years that I had worked in the health service that I had been off sick, even for a day. My staff simply couldn't believe it and I think they thought I must have had a terminal illness!

During that month I did go away for a week's holiday and I must say that I did feel slightly better at the end of it. The date when I left the service was set for June of that year and when the time came I was really glad to go. I never, ever thought that I would say that I was glad to leave the job I had loved.

There was one very happy occasion before I left. The staff arranged for a dinner which was attended not only by colleagues from across Northern Ireland but my mother and daughter as well. I had many lovely gifts including one from the Belfast Psychology Service. I would also like to mention one other gift in particular. The staff had paid a sum of money to the University of Ulster at Jordanstown to provide a prize each year for the student producing the best final year project. It was to be called the Eleanor Gildea Trophy. I later provided a rose bowl on which could be inscribed the names of the students.

There was to be one more surprise for me. At the end of the evening I was told to close my eyes. There was much laughter and cheering. I was told I could now open my eyes again. There in front of me tied up in ribbons and bows was my old green chair. A very lovely surprise! I took it home with me and continued to sit on it until I eventually retired from my charity work fourteen years later.

23

Post Resignation – Time to Relax

In November 1991 I received a very official looking document one morning, wondered what it was and upon opening it saw that it stated from Her Majesty Queen Elizabeth II *'to our trusted and beloved Mavis Eleanor Gildea'* and that, *'We have thought fit to nominate and appoint you to an Ordinary Member of the Civil Division of our said Most Excellent Order of the British Empire.'*

Words cannot express how I felt, I was overwhelmed. I don't think I could even express to you how my dear mother also felt. Of course we were not allowed to tell anyone apart from the immediate family, until the news was published at the beginning of the following January, in the New Year's Honours List. My mother, who normally never got up before eleven or eleven thirty each day, was downstairs that January morning at eight o'clock and the phone was red hot. I think she must have phoned everyone she knew to tell them about 'my Eleanor'.

There was great excitement over the next few months as we organized a hotel in London, my daughter and mother came with me of course and we all got new outfits for the day. I actually bought a pair of shoes that I think were a little too high so when I did my curtsy there was a distinct wobble.

On the day before the investiture we arrived in London,

my mother, my daughter and her husband came with me along with my two eldest grandchildren, Claire and Stephen. The following morning we called a taxi and when I said that we wanted to go to Buckingham Palace the driver was ecstatic. He had never been to Buckingham Palace in all his years of taxiing, he kept saying, "Just wait 'til I get home and tell the wife!"

As my mother was disabled and partially sighted we were actually allowed into the Palace grounds through the Duke of York gate. When we arrived two footmen came forward with a wheelchair and we were taken through to the ballroom where my mother and daughter had seats in the front row. Meanwhile I was in a large room being instructed, along with all the other people, in what to do. It was all very nerve-racking. I had to put a pin into my lapel before we met the Queen. As we came up to be presented someone called out, "Mavis Eleanor Gildea for services to speech therapy." I came up to the Queen and she asked me about my work, she then attached a medal to the pin in my lapel and I had to step back three paces and curtsy (plus wobble) and then move on out of the way for the next person.

At the end of the ceremony my mother decided that she didn't want to leave in a wheelchair, she said that she wanted to go with us and walk down the main staircase. We walked along a long corridor with many ante-rooms filled with beautiful paintings and we arrived at a magnificent staircase. On both sides there were, I think, members of the Household Cavalry stationed.

I must tell you of a very humorous incident that occurred. While my mother was coming down the right hand side of the staircase she was holding onto the banister for support and Valerie and I were walking beside her. Suddenly I heard my name. I turned round and saw my mother with her hand on a very delicate part of the soldier's body. She had come to the end of the banister and moved on. She called me when she was unable to find the banister again! I'm sorry to say Valerie and I could not keep from laughing. As I removed my mother's hand I apologized and as I looked at the soldier I'm sure that I could see a little gleam in his eye.

When I retired from the health service in 1991 one of the happiest times I spent was in babysitting two mornings a week for my grandchildren. My daughter, who is a GP, wanted to stay at home and mind the children and was thinking of giving up work as a doctor. However, I knew from personal experience that nobody can tell what will happen in the future and persuaded her that to give up her work at this stage would not be a good idea. She was happy to leave the children with me and so two mornings a week I went to her house to babysit. On my way there I would stop at the bakery 'The Golden Crumb'. This was the bakery where the owner gave me tray bakes and scones when I was fundraising. I collected iced fingers, jammy doughnuts or chocolate chip cookies. The order changed as the years went on. When the last child, Bethany, went to school I was only called on for my babysitting duties during the holidays. It was a very happy time.

24

A New Venture –
Action for Dysphasic Adults (NI)

I can't remember the exact date but sometime in the middle of
1990 I received a telephone call from a Mr John Travers Clarke.
John was retiring as the chairman of Action for Dysphasic
Adults, the national charity based in London. He told me that
he was anxious to do something for people with dysphasia
living in Northern Ireland. John's family had originally come
from here and his brother, who had continued to live in
Northern Ireland, had suffered from a speech problem. He told
me that he wanted to provide a donation of £5,000. He did not
mind how it was used as long as it related to people with
dysphasia. In view of all that was going on in the health services
in Northern Ireland at that time I told him that I would make
enquiries to see if I could find someone who would be
interested but in view of the circumstances I wasn't very
hopeful.

A few months later when I was considering whether I was
going to have my redundancy or not, I phoned John and
arranged to go to London to meet with him. I told him that I
wasn't sure what was happening but if I took my redundancy I
would be interested in taking up his offer.

At the beginning of 1991 when it was decided that I was able to take up the offer of redundancy, I contacted him again and put forward my proposals for the £5,000. I explained to him that from my earliest days in speech therapy I had always been interested in the use of intensive therapy. I proposed that I would use the £5,000 to run a four-week intensive course. John was very interested in this and was agreeable to provide the money when I required it.

My immediate problems regarding this were:

1. to find an experienced therapist who would be willing to do this course
2. to find volunteers as one therapist could not do this alone
3. to find the patients
4. to find accommodation

Regarding the first point, I was able to find an experienced therapist who was interested in what I was hoping to do. Her advice was to use students from the university. She thought they would be willing to do this as a part-time job during the summer holidays.

In terms of the third point, I contacted one of the consultants at the local hospital and he was very interested in the project and said that he would refer patients.

Lastly I also contacted the new Chief Executive of Down and Lisburn Trust, whom I had known for many years. The reason I chose this location was that John's family had come from that area. In the Down and Lisburn Trust they had just completed refurbishing a former restaurant in one of the hospitals and the Chief Executive allowed me to use this for the month of September.

The format was as follows: the patients would attend

everyday 9.30 a.m. to 3.30 p.m. Carers would have to give guarantee to attend one day each week. It was decided if the carer would not come then we would not take the patient. It is very important that carers understand the problems that people with aphasia experience.

To explain this I think it is very hard for lay people to understand what happens when a person is aphasic. I remember someone I knew from my golfing days whose husband had had a stroke. I met her one day and she was telling me about it and she was saying how difficult he had become since he had the stroke.

She kept saying, "He never does anything that I tell him to do, he just ignores me now. He's really very difficult, I find him very hard to put up with."

I must emphasize that this was many years ago and I don't think that he had seen a speech therapist at that time. As we stood in the car park that day I tried to explain to her that in all probability his comprehension had been affected by the stroke but she obviously didn't understand this. I think she just continued to shout at him!

The next thing we did, we invited applications from the students at the university. We interviewed them and six were accepted for the training course.

My first task was to visit the patients who had been referred. One of the first of these was Bill. He had been a successful businessman and was very, very frustrated at the limitations his aphasia had put on him. He was not totally without speech but had great word finding difficulty, reading and writing problems. He improved very well during the course and his family was very grateful for the service we provided. Bill joined the steering committee I set up in my home the following year and helped to draw up the constitution.

Another lady I met was Betty who also became a great supporter of the organisation. When I visited her and her husband prior to the course one thing she said stayed with me, it was something like, "We all look forward to our retirement and hope we'll have time to talk to each other and discuss things and suddenly Derek can't talk to me at all and it is very lonely here in the evenings."

I asked her if he communicated with her at all and her reply was, "Well if it's raining and I have the washing out he will come to the door and say, 'eh, eh' and I know that it's raining and I'd bring it in."

Derek was one of the people who made a great improvement during the course and I think was one of those that John Travers Clarke was most impressed by.

The third person I would like to mention is Liam. He had a stroke when I think he was in his late twenties. He was an engineering graduate and following his stroke and a right hemiplegia he was aphasic. He was a very keen sportsman and the paralysis was what initially caused him more problems than the lack of speech. He was determined that he would get back to playing football again. This he did and by the time I met him again he was coaching junior Gaelic football teams. Unfortunately because of his aphasia which affected his writing and numeracy abilities, he was unable to take up a post as an engineer. This was a great disappointment to him. He attended our first intensive course and following that was on our main committee and chairman of a local committee for many years. He was a great supporter of the charity and a great asset to the organisation.

I don't remember how anyone in Belfast heard about this

course but I suddenly started receiving phone calls asking if other people outside Downpatrick could attend. One woman in particular phoned me every week. I kept telling her that I would have to take ten patients from Downpatrick in the first instance but I think she was so keen for her husband to have this treatment that she just kept phoning.

I eventually went to meet with Margaret and her husband Eddie at their home. Margaret told me that Eddie had always been very calm and quiet and suddenly he was becoming quite aggressive. When I interviewed him I did meet a very, very angry man. He obviously had little if any comprehension, no speech at all. When I talked to him he just kept punching the air and in a very angry voice kept shouting, "No, no, no."

So I agreed to take him on the course. Both husband and wife became good friends and great supporters of the organisation. Another referral I added that day came from the Newtownards area. Rosemary rang about her husband Bertie who also had severe problems and again I agreed to take him.

The third man Joe was in his early forties and again had no speech. The only thing he ever said which he repeated frequently was, 'f***see'. Again his comprehension was severely limited.

September came and the course started and I have to say was a great success. Joe came from north Belfast and I arranged to meet him at a supermarket car park and take him. As we went to Downpatrick, if a heavy goods weight vehicle would drive past Joe would shout, 'f***see'. After four weeks of this I was nearly saying this myself! Eddie's temperament improved considerably as his comprehension improved and he started saying some words. The first words I heard him saying was as we drove one morning. There was a diversion and we ended up driving through a little village that we hadn't done before. Eddie suddenly looked over and said, "Orange Hall." I also heard from Margaret one day, one of the first things she heard Eddie say was, "Crow's feet." She thought it was very funny.

In the final week of the course we took all the patients and staff out for lunch at a nearby hotel. Joe was having a pint of Guinness and he was really enjoying himself. While his comprehension had improved, all I ever heard him say was 'f***see' which he said repeatedly as he drank. Nearby there were three 'mature ladies' having their lunch. As Joe went on with his talking I could gradually see their backs stiffening as they sat up in their chairs. I went over to the ladies, explained that Joe had had a severe stroke and was not swearing. That was all he could say.

They were very understanding and said, "That's alright love. We don't mind at all."

On the final day of the course John Travers Clarke came over to meet with the patients, carers and the staff. He spent the whole afternoon talking with them and at the end of the afternoon he said how delighted he was at the results.

He said, "Eleanor, if I gave you half the amount £2,500, do you think you could raise the rest and do another course next year?"

I said, "Yes, I think I could."

Hence the beginning of 'Action for Dysphasic Adults Northern Ireland', eventually to become 'Speech Matters'.

I set up my office in a bedroom in my home. Someone gave me a typewriter which I couldn't use and I bought a filing cabinet. I started to think where I could run the next course and decided that Lisburn would be a good venue. During the next number of months I again had to find additional funding, a venue and another speech therapist. I think the Trust provided part of the money for the course.

I would like to mention my mother here. Mother had come to live with me after Jack died as she was no longer able to cope in her own home. She was almost blind, had severe osteoporosis, was asthmatic and had diverticulitis among other problems. She was delighted that I was working from home. When people phoned up and I wasn't there my mother really enjoyed talking to them and when I returned home she would tell me their story. This really gave her a tremendous interest during the day. However, as my mother couldn't really see the phone number that she was writing down for me sometimes it was almost illegible.

I just reminded her, "If someone phones, tell them if I don't ring back, they have to ring again. Explain to them that you cannot see."

Next thing was that I had to get a call minder to enable me to keep a record of anyone who had phoned.

Regarding referrals for the course, I contacted local consultants and got very good support. I don't know how it happened but I remember doing an interview on the radio one morning about this course and following that was quite surprised to receive referrals and enquires from both Scotland and England. I explained to both these enquiries that there would have to be some form of payment because the Trust was unable to fund anyone outside its own area and this was agreed. We eventually ended up with a man from Scotland whose wife flew over once a week to attend the carers' course. On her return to Scotland she campaigned to have similar courses started there. Regarding the woman from England, I managed to find accommodation for herself and her husband who stayed in Northern Ireland for the four weeks.

Unfortunately our original speech therapist was unable to come. I contacted the London organisation for ADA and was put in touch with Jane, who came over. She ran an excellent course. Jane and I have remained very good friends ever since.

So to tell you a little bit about some of these people. Catherine was very elegant and always beautifully dressed. I remember one day I had gone to Lisburn and I was having lunch with the patients and staff. We were talking about what was going to happen that afternoon at the course and the therapists said, "We are going to have a quiz today."

At this point Catherine gave a little cough and said, "Oh shit."

To say that everyone fell into fits of laughter would be putting it mildly. It was such an unexpected remark for her to make! Another lady who attended had had a stroke when she was in her forties. She had some speech but her biggest problem was that she was suffering from severe depression. When she came she was in a wheelchair, wearing a tracksuit, wore no make-up and her hair was long and unkempt. There was another very small lady who came, both came from opposite sides of the community and both became great friends. It was great to see little Avril pushing Betty around in her wheelchair.

On the last week of the course, Betty arrived one day in her wheelchair wearing a very nice dress, her hair had been cut and she was wearing make-up. What a transformation! A number of weeks after the course, Betty's husband had raised money in West Belfast and there was a lovely photograph, which appeared in the local papers, taken of her presenting the cheque to me. She was very proud of this moment. She continued to improve both with her speech and walking. I met Betty some years later and was delighted to see that her speech was almost normal and she was walking very well.

The course in Lisburn was very successful and I decided that I would continue to do this but the money would have to be raised by myself because there was no more money coming from John.

Following the course I decided that the best way to do this was to set up a charity. I obviously needed some help. I didn't know anything about setting up a charity but I realized that would need to find a committee, draw up a constitution and ultimately I was going to need premises.

I was very fortunate in finding a consultant in the Belfast City Hospital who said that he would be very happy to come onto the committee. I was very lucky to find him, he was most supportive and was able to look up other constitutions and provide advice. I also contacted a patient, Bill, who had been on the first intensive course. Bill had a friend who was a retired GP. They agreed to meet every few weeks and the four of us would meet at my house to draw up the constitution. I acquired a secretary who would come in one morning a week to do some typing. If I needed any typing done other than that I would write it all out in longhand, take it down to a secretary I had at my clinic twenty years prior to this, she would type it and leave it for me to collect later. At that time I worked about six hours a week on the charity's business and once every three months I would go over to a meeting of the national charity in London.

One of the ways I thought of raising money was to actually charge for attendance. GPs at that time were fund holders and would be able to provide the £500 we charged for the course. In order to do this we would have to set up some form of contract and when I was at one of the meetings in London I discovered that staff there couldn't help me in terms of drawing up a contract because unfortunately the national charity provided advice and information only.

Once I had drawn up the constitution I wrote to NICVA (Northern Ireland Council for Voluntary Action) asking if the constitution would be accepted and if Action for Dysphasic Adults NI could be registered as an official charity. I eventually received word that with a few minor alterations, the constitution was accepted and was registered as a charity.

Our third course was held in Bangor. By this time I had a committee for the charity and also a group of carers who were very supportive and did some fundraising for the organisation.

By this time my bedroom was getting overcrowded. The bed was still in it but I had now acquired a computer (which I couldn't use), a filing cabinet and a table on which to write my letters. I decided that it was time I found accommodation for the charity.

The other big issue that came up was that the carers felt that they would like somewhere for the people with aphasia to meet each week, so finding premises where we could do this was essential. It's hard to remember but I think that it was probably at the beginning of 1994 that I acquired premises in Knockbracken Healthcare Park (formerly Purdysburn Hospital). Initially I rented one small office and a large room where the patients could come once a week and where we could have our monthly carers' group meetings.

This carers' group was very good. Once a month they organized various fundraising activities: a Burns Night and a storytelling night amongst others. Once we were established as a charity I was able to apply to the DHSS for a grant. These grants were first given out in 1990 and related to the level of provision which a charity was providing. Unfortunately Action for Dysphasic Adults (NI) was not set up officially until 1993 and therefore could not be related to our level of provision. I think we were eventually awarded £11,000 per annum. The rest of our funding came from GPs providing it for their patient, patients providing their own funding or from fundraising.

I have to pay tribute here first of all to a friend, Fred, who I'm sure won't mind me mentioning the work he did in keeping the books for the charity. I think I was the bane of his existence, in fact I know I was! I was always optimistic that money would come in to pay the staff that we ultimately acquired and Fred was equally pessimistic that we would go into the red. Following Fred's resignation I called on my cousin Bob who did the books for many years.

When I acquired the premises in Knockbracken Healthcare Park I decided that I would offer one or two, maybe even three, intensive courses per year. I would then have trained assistants and together with a speech therapist we would run groups in Knockbracken once or twice a week.

I advertised for the assistants and initially had something like 35 applications. The speech therapist who was to run the course and I met most of the applicants for a full afternoon at Knockbracken. Following that a smaller number were offered individual interviews. Six people were then offered the training. The training ran for two full weeks, 9.30 a.m. until 3.30 p.m. everyday and we hoped to be able to employ all six of those we had trained. However, at the end of the course one woman decided that while she loved the work the one thing she could not do would be to take a man to the toilet. We all understood.

It is very hard after this length of time to remember the exact sequence of events but the intensive courses ran very well, we always had the full complement of patients and as time went by I started to expand the number of groups. I opened groups in Bangor, Lisburn, Coleraine, Londonderry, Strabane, Banbridge, Cookstown, Belfast and Newtownabbey. I ended up with thirteen in total. From an administrative point of view, there were many pamphlets and information leaflets to be written. In addition to the constitution I had to draw up a Health and Safety policy, a policy for the Protection of Vulnerable Adults and I had to produce annual reports which had to go to the Department of Health to ensure our continued core funding.

When I started the aphasia groups it was because I felt very strongly that it was not right that people with aphasia were being placed in day centres where the majority of the people were able to communicate. I am sure there would be questions asked if someone who could not speak English was placed in a day centre without an interpreter being with them. Yet we do this with our stroke patients.

Following on from this I realized that shops in towns displayed signs showing that the staff were trained in how to communicate with anyone who was deaf. So my shop scheme was initiated. I contacted supermarkets and stores in various towns, Belfast, Bangor, L'Derry, especially in places where we had our groups. I offered to train the staff in how to help anyone who had a communication disorder. The training lasted about one and a half hours and we had a very good response, only one supermarket refused to participate. I gave the shops a Speech Matters Logo sticker to display on their entrance doors.

I also arranged for a card to be printed for our members, it said one of the following:

I have had a stroke

I am unable to speak

I speak very slowly

The name of the charity and contact information was printed on the other side of the card.

The members were very pleased with these cards, especially the women. They felt that they could now do their shopping with confidence and that they would no longer be embarrassed.

It would be worthwhile to tell you at this time about some of those we treated during the years. A few people I remember very well. One of my very favourite people I met during this time was called Paul. His wife had heard me speaking on the radio one morning and phoned to ask if there was anything I could do to help him. He had had a stroke when he was six years old, he had never learnt to read or write. He had a paralysed arm and had trouble with his right leg. He had always had a very poorly paid job, usually as a caretaker. I met Paul and his wife and arranged for him to attend our intensive course. He and his wife, Bernie, told us how they had met just a few years previously. Paul had gone down to Dublin to a dance and had asked someone to partner him and she had refused. Bernie was standing by and told him that she would dance with him and the rest, as they say, is history. They arranged to meet again and a very short time later, they were married. They were an absolutely delightful couple. When the course was over, I received a letter from Paul which said something like:

Dear Eleanor,

This is the first letter I ever wrote, and I wanted you to have it. Thank you for having me on the course.

Love,

Paul.

Despite all his physical problems, Paul was a charming man. I remember one night we were having a 'race' meeting as a fundraiser and at one stage I think they were selling the horses and Paul kept bidding. Sometimes he would bid again even if his bid was the last one in. We would say, "Paul! You've won, stop bidding!"

He would always say, "Oh well, have another bid anyway! It's a good cause!"

Unfortunately, this story has a sad ending; Bernie died a few years later. Paul was desolate and shortly after that he had another stroke. I went to visit him. He was probably in his late forties at that time and was in a ward with people many years older than he was. I came out feeling very depressed. I lost touch with Paul after that as I understand that he was moved to another hospital and died shortly after that.

Pauline was only about 19 years old when she took a stroke. She was married and had a young baby. While stroke units had been set up a few years earlier in Northern Ireland, for some curious reason they had been set up in geriatric units in hospitals. So if you had a stroke and were young, you would find that people were much older than you were. Pauline was eventually sent to day care and she used to return home everyday to her husband and mother, crying and saying, "All 90, all 90." Pauline was referred to our intensive course and improved considerably. Her family, who had been very concerned about the depression that she was experiencing, were delighted. Following the intensive course Pauline attended our client group each week. Her mother and the extended family were very supportive of the organisation.

Another young girl who attended the intensive course had been a very high flying secretary. Two of her brothers had strokes and both of these had resulted from congenital aneurisms. Neither of her brothers had any residual paralysis. The consultants decided that Deirdre's aneurism should be corrected in case she too had a stroke. Unfortunately following the operation, she did have slight paralysis and became aphasic. She too came on one of our intensive courses and attended the client group.

Richard attended one of our courses. He had had a stroke when he was in his forties. He had been very much an academic and suddenly most of the pastimes he enjoyed were no longer possible. He could read, but very slowly, his comprehension was impaired as was his speech. Richard came with me a few times when I was fundraising. It is very difficult for lay people to understand the problems people have when they become aphasic. Richard was able to explain these problems very slowly. One of these problems, because he lived on his own, was dealing with money. His friends were very good and always ensured that 'large' shopping was done by them, but for day-to-day shopping for things like milk or newspapers, there was a problem. Richard's way of solving this was to keep only pound coins in his pocket. So when he went into a shop where they knew him and purchased his paper or milk, or what he needed, he would come over the counter and start putting coins down one at a time. If the assistant said something like £7.90, he would keep putting down one pound after another until he got to eight. He was then told by the assistant that he had enough. It was very hard for Richard, who had enjoyed reading, good conversation, going to the theatre and all these things were no longer possible. I sometimes wondered how he kept so cheerful.

On the theme of money I remembered a carer who came to us. Her husband had a farm and all their married life he had dealt with all their finances relating to the farm and to the home. She told me that each week her husband had given her 'pay' and she used this to buy groceries and items for the home, if she needed money to buy clothes, she would ask him and he would give her a little extra. Following his stroke she was faced with dealing with the farm and all the finances that entailed. Her neighbours had rallied around and helped with the farm but finances proved to be beyond her. I remembered her saying, "Eleanor, I've got a letter here about rates, what are rates? They want me to send a cheque and I've never written a cheque in my life, what do I do?"

She lived a considerable distance from Belfast so I suggested that I would contact the social services department and that someone would come and help her to deal with her financial affairs. She was horrified at this idea. Someone from social services, she felt, would imply that she didn't have any money and that she was looking for help and this was something, in her eyes, of a disgrace. Ultimately I organized for our social worker to go up and spend some time with her. I also arranged for her to see her bank manager. I was glad to say that we were able to sort out most of her problems.

One other person I remember very well was called Sean. Sean also had a massive stroke when he was about forty. He had a young family. Following the stroke he had no speech and was unable to walk. He too was in a geriatric unit. His wife was campaigning tirelessly to get him into a rehabilitation unit in England but unfortunately funding was not available. When she heard about our services, she phoned me to see if he could attend. The problem was that they lived about fifty miles from Belfast and to attend everyday for four weeks would have been impossible. However, where there's a will there's a way, and Sean's wife eventually managed to find a friend who lived nearer who was willing to let Sean stay during the week and just go home at weekends.

On the Friday before the start of our intensive courses we always had a get together of staff, patients and carers. This was not only to let the participants meet each other but to show them round the premises and let them know arrangements about food etc. I well remember the Friday that Sean attended with his wife. He came in slumped in his wheelchair, looking very dejected. We had quite a few young people on our course that year. A few days later on the Wednesday morning I was sitting in my office. At 8.30 a.m., I heard a tapping outside. My office was isolated and I wondered what this noise was. I got up and looked out and there coming down the corridor, walking with the aid of a stick, was Sean. I couldn't believe it. I think what had happened was Sean was so depressed at being with so many older people with physical disabilities and probably thought that this would be him in the future. When he came to the course with younger people, all with similar disabilities, he could see them walking and many of them also talking. His whole attitude had changed. I could not explain how delighted his wife was.

One day his wife told me that her son had said, "Mummy I wish I had my daddy back."

She explained to him that he would only be gone for a few

179

weeks while the course was on and then his daddy would come back.

The boy said, "No, I want my old daddy back, the one who could talk."

I realised at that time that we really had given very little thought to the children of our patients with aphasia and how they were affected. Two things happened following that. I applied to the Lottery for funding to purchase books that had been published by Action for Dysphasic Adults called, 'When Granny Couldn't Talk'. I received the funding and had these books distributed to all speech therapists in Northern Ireland and a few years after that my husband made a video talking to children about how they had been affected by their parent's stroke.

A few years after starting the charity I sat down to consider what the deficiencies were in the present service to the aphasic population in Northern Ireland. I decided that I would try to address each one of these deficiencies through our organisation. The issue of intensive therapy was already being addressed in our courses. The need for client groups was also being addressed. My next objective was to obtain someone to do the counselling and advocacy.

I was very fortunate to obtain funding for a social worker and got a wonderful girl called Sharon. Over the years and before I left, I acquired two more social workers to carry out this valuable service across the province.

In 1997 I went on a holiday, a bus tour of Georgia and the Carolinas. The day I left my mother was taken into hospital. I kept in touch by phone each day and five days later I was told that my mother needed an operation and that she wouldn't have it until I came home. I cancelled the rest of the holiday and flew back to Belfast. I arrived two days later and went up to the hospital. Mother had the operation that afternoon.

She responded well at first and then the wound opened and she had a further operation. Unfortunately the doctors were unable to do anything for her. She died ten weeks later having put up a very brave fight. She was eighty-seven years old.

Every year the national organisation ran the Diana Law Memorial Lecture in honour of its founder and it was pleased to fund the person giving the lecture to come to Northern Ireland and speak to our patients and carers.

After some years the two charities, the one in London and the one in Belfast were offering very different services and both changed their names. The national charity become 'Speakability' and we renamed ours 'Speech Matters'.

The national charity then decided that it would no longer pay for the lecturer's expenses and I decided to pay these myself. I called it the Jane Hutchinson Memorial Lecture in honour of my mother. She would have loved it.

I remember someone asking me, "Who was Jane Hutchinson?" I explained that she was my mother and how she had devoted her life to caring for her mother who had been completely disabled for twenty-five years and then for her father. I also told them of the help, support and love she had always given to my family and me.

One year the person giving the lecture was called Barbara Newborn. She had written a book entitled *Return to Ithica*. Barbara had a massive stroke when she was twenty-one, a few months after graduating from college. She had a right-side hemiplegia and unfortunately no speech at all. How she regained her speech is outlined in her book. It is a truly inspirational story.

A few months following her lecture here, she wrote to me to say that there was to be a large conference in New York in June. This was to be attended by eminent neurologists from across America. She wanted me to come and talk about the services I was currently offering in Northern Ireland. This invitation was a great surprise to me. I considered it and decided that I would go and take Sharon with me.

The conference at the Columbian Medical Centre lasted for two days and both Sharon and I got a very warm reception. One of the speakers following my talk was also a speech pathologist. The title of her talk was, 'My Vision for Speech Therapy in the 21st Century'.

She started her lecture by saying, "I don't know what to say because it appears that my vision for speech therapy in America in the 21st century is already being done in Northern Ireland today." I was very, very flattered.

One very important aspect of the service was the work we did with carers and I am including some examples from letters we received.

It helped my husband enormously. He's learned how to take his time whenever he wants to communicate and it helped him cope with the terrible frustration. By the end of the course he was a much happier man.
Edna

My husband enjoyed meeting the group and the informality of the sessions with the therapists. He even enjoyed doing the homework! There has definitely been an improvement and he has a lot more confidence in himself. He made a phone call recently and this was the first time in eight years.
Jacqueline

I found the training days for the relatives a great benefit. I passed on the information to my family and we are now more tolerant as we have a better understanding of his affliction.

Lora

I cannot get over how well his speech has improved since the course and he now attends the day centre twice a week.

Betty

My father learned how to do many things for himself. One very important one being how to use gesture if he couldn't say what he wanted to. This had helped him to regain his confidence and lessen his frustration.

Isobel

One thing I am especially thankful for is what the course did for me and my family. It gave me back my sanity. Before, I could not understand what had happened or how I could help my father. Then at last someone explained.

Rosemary

I continued to run training courses every year for both patients and carers. One year we ran three courses, Belfast, Draperstown and Banbridge, each attended by approximately forty people. That was the year we had the Equality and Human Rights Commissions. We trained some staff from both these organisations in how to communicate with people with aphasia and so these important pieces of legislation were made available to people who would otherwise not have understood what was going on. During the time of the 'Good Friday Agreement', staff spent considerable time explaining this to all our members.

We found the police service in Northern Ireland were very helpful in these times and would often provide transport for patients and carers to bring them to these venues.

The charity gradually expanded until we had twenty-four staff including a secretary, part-time fundraiser, social workers, one full-time speech therapist, a number of part-time assistants and I had a part-time deputy who, like me, would spend about twelve hours per week on charity business. I think we eventually, before I left, had a turnover every year of approximately £345,000. It was a wonderful, exciting time and so good to bring help and support to so many people.

In the millennium year a change was to come. I met George and the following year we got married. This decision was a surprise to both of us as when we met we both said that we did not want to get married again. George's wife had died six years previously. However, we changed our minds. A few years later, I think it was in 2003 I decided that I had worked long enough and I really wanted to spend my time with George. I decided to resign.

The next few years were very happy, we both enjoyed golf and we spend many holidays cruising the high seas. One very memorable holiday was when we spent seven weeks in the Caribbean.

Unfortunately this happy time did not last. George became very ill and died in March 2009. He was a gentle, kind and loving man. A great loss and I miss him very much.

25

Conclusion

My late husband George used to say when I told him about my work, "You should write that down." One day he actually took me out and bought me a recorder to enable me to dictate my story. I used to see the dictaphone sitting there and I would remember his words.

Unfortunately my eyesight is now poor. If I start to write something down I always write again over the previous line. I had never learned to use a computer. When I started to use the dictaphone the problem was I never was sure whether I had pressed the button to record or the button to delete.

One day I had a great idea – I would enlist the help of a grandchild. So my grandson Gareth volunteered to type my story into my computer. I dictated and he typed. When Gareth had to stop due to his work commitments, I found another typist (a student, Frances) and she completed the typing task.

As I am sitting here now reading my book I remember so many more of my patients and their families. I remember their stories, their worries and their fears and I also remember the funny times as well.

I will finish this book with a final amusing story. One year my family and I were going on a package holiday to Gran

Canaria. Suddenly I looked over the plane and saw the mother of one of my patients. She saw me at the same time. "Hello Mrs Shaw," she shouted, "just to let you know Jimmy is back in jail again – he only got six months this time, burglary as usual. You remember the last time they let him out early, hope they keep him in this time. Have a good holiday, see you when you come home."

As I felt the glances of those around me all I could do was smile and say, "Enjoy your holiday, see you soon."